MANAGING
INFORMAL EMPLOYEE
ORGANIZATIONS

FRANK W. SHAW JD, PHD

ISBN: 1481207520
ISBN-13: 9781481207522

Library of Congress Control Number: 2012923353
CreateSpace Independent Publishing Platform North Charleston,
South Carolina

CONTENTS

PREFACE

In 1938, Chester Barnard published his classic book, *Functions of the Executive*, in which he discussed, among other things, the informal organizations that spontaneously spring up within every formal organization. These informal organizations provide the social structure that governs how the company's employees actually work together and respond to management. Although informal organizations are not planned or formalized in policies or organizational charts, they exert profound influence on the behavior, interactions, norms, motivations, relationships, and perceptions of those who work within them. The systems of these informal organizations are notoriously difficult to manage because they are based on emotions rather than rational thinking. This book describes the nature of these information organizations and provides techniques for effectively managing them.

Every company consists of a formal organization and any number of informal organizations. The formal organization is the result of planning and is deliberately designed to accomplish its intended purpose as efficiently as possible. The leadership structure of the formal organization is bound together by codified rules and policies. It is organized hierarchically from the top down, it equates people with their roles, and it is observable. The rational origin of the formal organization makes it easily understood and amenable to alteration through the planning processes of management. When people think of a company or any other type of organization, they typically think of the formal aspects of that organization.

Informal organizations, on the other hand, evolve organically from the social interactions of their members and continue to change along with environmental factors in the workplace. Members of informal organizations relate to each other in accord with the unwritten and often unspoken opinions held by coworkers. The informal leadership structure is based upon perceived status differences among the members of the group rather than job description. It is not easily observable by outsiders, tends to be flat rather than hierarchical, and is maintained largely by the social relationships of its members. The support of informal organizations is essential when formal organizations find themselves in crisis or environments characterized by rapid change.

The social dynamics of informal organizations have long been recognized as complex, non-rational, and subject to frequent fluctuations arising from changes in the work environment. They are not the product of poor management or planning and cannot be eliminated or ignored. They have the power to contribute to the formal structures, strategies, and functions of an organization, or to destroy them. They can be sources of innovation, strength, support, and resiliency during crises, or they can be reservoirs of resistance to change, defiance of authority, inefficiency, and sabotage. In short, well-managed informal organizations dramatically improve the functioning of the formal organizations to which they are attached while those that are poorly managed or ignored reduce productivity, impose unnecessary psychological burdens on their members and management, and ultimately hamstring the entire organization

Managers interacting with the informal organizations within their companies often feel that, ideally, informal organizations would not exist if their companies were organized cleverly enough. This view is the product of mystification and frustration. In reality, informal organizations are not byproducts of inept planning or organizational structuring at all. They inevitably grow within all formal organizations and cannot be avoided, ignored or eliminated. Managers who recognize this are in a unique position to capitalize on the combined power of their formal and informal organizations by integrating employee interests with company objectives. This integration of goals involves building solutions to company problems that are based upon Mary Parker Follett's "law of the situation" rather than domination or compromise to produce higher morale, improved job satisfaction, and increased efficiency. Skillful management of informal organizations unleashes the potential for creative innovation like nothing else in the manager's tool box.

However, as the writers of the classic books on management asked, how specifically does one go about managing informal organizations? This book is devoted to presenting surprisingly simple and eminently practical answers to this question. While most authorities agree that the key to managing all organizations is communication, they stop short of describing exactly how this crucial communication can be established and maintained. Employee education and shared management programs have not been as effective as some have hoped. The fault lies not in the design of these approaches or in their execution, but in the fact that they are rationally based rather than emotionally based. Informal organizations, as opposed to formal organizations, are grounded in emotion and do not respond to the economic logic and planning processes of management.

This book is not intended to provide a comprehensive review of the vast literature dealing with the techniques and strategies that managers are currently using in the workplace. References to the classics of management are provided in support of the ideas presented to provide a sense of history and to acknowledge the contributions of great managers and industrial psychologists. Source material is included to develop the reasoning behind the processes discussed and to provide interested managers with the rationale necessary to garner support for improving communication within their departments and plants.

It is the intent of this work to provide practical techniques for managing the informal systems operating within any type of company. The effective use of these techniques presupposes the careful planning by management that produces viable businesses. In the absence of a viable formal organizational structure, informal organizations perish. Nevertheless, planning and other work products of the formal managerial processes of organizations cannot, by themselves, produce the changes in employee attitudes necessary for optimal efficiency.

It is hoped that providing concrete descriptions of processes that are effective in engaging informal organizations will make the processes themselves more accessible to busy managers. These activities will improve communication and engage employees even in hostile environments. In fact, their effects are most dramatic in dysfunctional working environments because they allow managers to deal with the real problems rather than merely the symptoms. The skillful management of informal organizations will improve the quality of life for both employees and managers while increasing the efficiency and productivity of the companies within which they have evolved.

1.

THE COMPLEX WORKPLACE

Managers in modern business organizations are faced with a myriad of complex problems. In many respects, however, they are better prepared to meet the challenges of their profession than ever before. Theoretical and experimental knowledge of management has progressed dramatically since the turn of the century when Frederick Winslow Taylor introduced scientific management to optimistic business owners and suspicious workers. The expansion of MBA programs in colleges and universities is evidence of the widespread confidence placed in these programs by the business community.

Despite the theoretical, technical, and planning knowledge acquired by managers, they often find themselves in relatively hostile environments where the people they are charged to lead rebel and sabotage their efforts to increase efficiency. When managers are confronted by suspicious, unmotivated employees, they immediately are made aware of the gaps in their knowledge of the social and psychological realities of the workplace. It was only to be expected that the critical problems confronting managers is in the area of human relations. The major difficulty encountered by managers with the people they supervise is often described as the "natural resistance" they seem to have to any sort of change.[1]

One unfortunate result of the frustrations experienced by managers trying to work with employees has been the development of the widespread belief that the interests of employees and

---

1   Armand Feigenbaum, *Total Quality Control* (New York: McGraw-Hill, Inc., 1991), 193.

employers are necessarily antagonistic. This belief is especially interesting in light of the fact that scientific management was historically based on the idea that employee/employer interests were ultimately the same: Employers cannot succeed unless their employees succeed and vice versa.

When a company is properly managed, both groups' interests are addressed.[2] When employees do not feel that their special interests are consistent with those of the company, trouble can be expected. For example, Frederick Winslow Taylor's innovations in the area of scientific management were strongly opposed by organized labor when his ideas were perceived as inconsistent with the best interests of employees. The resistance of organized labor to scientific management stemmed from its reliance on the skillful application of sustainable incentives to improve employee performance.

Scientific management increased productivity by increasing employee compensation. Employees shared in the economic benefits of increased efficiency. The problems that arose in companies attempting to apply scientific management were the result of poor management, greed, and the employees' fear that once productivity had increased, their companies would stop paying the incentives and insist that they do more work for less pay. Concern regarding the dilution of incentives has been generally justified by widespread business practices in America. Employers have routinely diluted incentives or abandoned them altogether once productivity has increased.

The use of economic incentives presents serious problems of design and morale that are very difficult to resolve. Nevertheless, the belief persists that economic incentives are the answer to increasing employee performance and overall morale despite longstanding and well-documented proof to the contrary. It is actually well known within the management community that eco-

---

2   Frederick Winslow Taylor, *The Principles of Scientific Management* (New York: Harper & Row, 1911).

nomic incentives by themselves are ineffective and, in some work environments, even counterproductive.

In the early 1900s, Frederick Winslow Taylor, the father of scientific management, estimated that the average employee routinely works somewhere between one-half and one-third capacity. His estimate is not out of line in most American companies today. If employees attempt to do any more than this, they run the risk of the disapproval of their fellow employees. Taylor referred to deliberately working below capacity as "soldiering" and suggested that it was almost universal in industries around the world in his time. To address this issue, he advocated "intimate cooperation" between management and employees. In situations where employees support management, companies can expect the average daily output of each person to nearly double.[3]

What is very important here is the recognition that employees have the power independent of management to increase or decrease efficiency in the workplace. This power comes from the social networks that have evolved within their companies. Chester Barnard, one of the great contributors to modern management theory, was the first to recognize this and referred to these social networks of employees as "informal organizations." His work drew attention to the existence and the power of these networks.

In light of Barnard's work, it is clear today that a focus on appropriate incentives only partially addresses the problems facing managers who are striving to increase the efficiency of their businesses. Although managers have long been aware that social and psychological issues need to be addressed in the workplace, there has been very little work to determine just how this may be done other than by offering economic incentives. Most American companies design themselves to perform at levels lower than their potential simply because managers do not know how to manage the informal employee organizations within their departments, or they simply do not know these powerful organizations exist.

3   Ibid., 5-6.

Three causes for the deliberate inefficiency of employees are frequently cited in management literature: (a) the belief of employees that increasing their efficiency will result in the loss of jobs; (b) the widespread existence of compensation practices that encourage soldiering to protect employee interests; and, (c) inefficient "rule-of-thumb" methods that waste a great deal of worker effort.[4] Taylor advocated scientific management as a means of arriving at solutions to these problems. In spite of the revolutionary success of this approach to management and its widespread application in companies over the last hundred years, these problems have not been eradicated. The intransigence of these problems comes from the inability of most managers to develop successful informal employee organizations within their businesses.

To be sure, scientifically measuring performance and carefully designing work environments and machines have improved productivity in the workplace. However, systematic soldiering originates with the social relationships among the employees themselves. The widespread prevalence of employees working below capacity and taking adversarial attitudes toward management in companies today illustrates the power of informal organizations.[5] A review of the classic literature of management reveals that although awareness of this power has gradually increased since the turn of the century, most managers remain painfully inept at managing informal organizations.

There are likely many reasons this area of management has progressed so slowly, but the complexity of the workplace is certainly at least partially responsible. The complexities of modern companies present serious challenges for researchers. A good case in point is Elton Mayo, one of the earliest and foremost contributors to the literature of industrial psychology. In the thirties, Mayo became interested in searching for ways to make the workplace more efficient through experimentation. In designing his experiments, he noticed that due to the complexity of working

---

4   Ibid., 7.
5   Taylor, *The Principles of Scientific Management*, 10.

environments and social relationships typical cause-effect analysis could lead to erroneous conclusions.

Such a simple approach to Mayo's studies was impracticable due to the mutual dependence among the variables that affect workers' performance.[6] Mayo's acknowledgement of this dependence ultimately contributed to his discovery of what has become known as the Hawthorne Effect. This effect, resulting from the attitudes and opinions of the employees themselves, was found to have more influence on productivity and employee support than any other variable studied. In short, he learned that employee performance is influenced more by employee attitudes than any other variables or even cluster of variables.

The power of employee attitudes toward their work and toward management can be harnessed to support organizational goals or can act as an insurmountable obstacle to the achievement of almost any organizational improvement whatsoever. Although Mayo believed the mystery of this power was due to some form of disequilibrium within the organization or the individual, he was the first to discover and prove experientially that the awesome power and influence of informal organizations of employees exists within practically every company.[7]

In the 1940s, Chester Barnard made considerable progress in developing the concept of employees' social networks and described companies as consisting of both formal and informal organizations. He conceived of formal organizations as systems of consciously coordinated activities planned and coordinated by managers.[8] The official organization of a company includes its organizational charts, intended lines of authority, policies, evaluation systems, and economy of incentives. These formal aspects of companies are designed and maintained by managers.

---

6   Elton, Mayo, *The Human Problems of an Industrial Civilization*, 2nd ed. (Cambridge: Division of Research, Graduate School of Business Administration, Harvard University Press, 1946), 11-12.

7   Ibid. 26.

8   Chester Barnard, *The Functions of the Executive*, 13th anniversary ed. (Cambridge: Harvard University Press, 1968), 73.

The formal organization of every company in business, however, exists side by side with related, informal organizations that have evolved within it. These employee social networks comprise all of the personal interactions and associated relationships of the employees working within the departmental divisions of their companies. Despite the lack of a planned structure, informal organizations have considerable impact on the functioning of the companies within which they exist.

Every formal organization, whether business, educational, religious, military, or governmental, is associated with one or more informal organizations of employees that exert powerful influences on the intended functioning of the formal organizations within which they have evolved.[9] Successful executives facilitate the reconciliation of conflicting forces, instincts, interests, and ideals between management and employees.[10] A key role of managers is the coordination of the formal and informal organizations within the enterprises they manage.

Managing the emotional reactions of employees within the working environment is not a simple matter. Most managers are unaware of or only have a passing familiarity with the existence and power of social networks among their employees, which foster the ability to communicate with one another seemingly without notice and with amazing speed; this is often referred to as "the grapevine." This is due to a remarkable lack of information regarding informal organizations in management textbooks and popular business literature. The functioning of informal organizations simply has not received as much attention as other aspects of organizational behavior.

The situation is made more complex for managers due to their own emotional reactions to the situations they encounter. Managers attempting to apply their expertise to dysfunctional groups of employees are typically frustrated by the irrational

---

9   Barnard, *The Functions of the Executive*, 115.
10   Ibid., 21.

reactions of their employees. When managers address emotional employee groups, they are often put in situations for which they have had very little training, and their own emotional reactions actually get in the way of making decisions rationally.

Decision-making is and has always been a critical function of management. A manager's experience and judgment are called upon in everything from dealing with routine operating problems to crafting and revising major policies. Rarely, however, does the manager know all of the relevant facts needed for making the most effective decision. In practice, the idea that managers gather all the facts, weigh them, and then make their decisions based on a complete understanding of them is rarely accurate.

In reality, the available facts gathered are usually incomplete due to the time constraints imposed by the urgency of the most pressing situation. In addition, the complex nature of rapidly changing conditions, and the resulting inferences, opinions, emotions, and a host of other subjective factors, play surprisingly important roles. Decisions are influenced by considerably more than just the facts.

Regardless of good intentions and the time spent on the decision-making process, managers know that the responsibility for the final decision and its consequences falls directly on them. This pressure works against managers by motivating them to make decisions without employee input. Allowing employees who will not share in the consequences of a poor decision to help make it simply does not make sense to most managers when confronted with situations they feel are capable of producing serious consequences. This results in poorer decisions and strained relationships with employees.

The fact that managers must consider the feelings of their people further adds to the complexity of managerial decision-making. If they fail to make this consideration, their employees' negative reactions will soon bring this to their attention. Managers dealing with angry employees are very likely to become angry themselves.

Managers' emotions nearly always influence their decisions and, in some situations, can be paramount.

When managers feel as though certain situations are threatening their pride or position in the organization, they tend to make decisions based on strong emotional reactions as a form of face-saving or in an attempt to protect management in general, and often because of their fear of change. Although we are all aware of how challenging it is to avoid being misled by emotional considerations, sooner or later, we all make mistakes. When these mistakes occur, the resistance of subordinates is severe and debilitating to the organization. Interestingly, unsupportive, hostile, and suspicious employee social networks very often pose threats to managers that result in very poor, emotionally based decisions.

With this in mind, what can a manager do when he or she is compelled to deal with a dysfunctional group of employees? Unilateral decisions will only produce poor results and lead to further strained relations with employees. This creates a vicious circle in which employees react negatively to the manager and the manager reciprocates with his or her own negative reaction to subordinates, which results in poor decisions that further stress the employee-management relationship.

Without a practical answer to this question, managers have been counseled to focus on avoiding situations that are likely to cost them the support of their employees. Nearly all of the management literature recommends that managers seek and accept feedback from subordinates and allow them to participate in the decision-making processes to the fullest extent possible. The literature further promises the good will and support of the employees involved when this practice is followed. Of course, this is more easily said than done, especially when subordinates offer suggestions that are in opposition to the manager's views or are clearly self-serving and seemingly counter to the best interests of the organization.

When employees resist management, the resulting stress makes it difficult for managers to give opposing views a sympathetic hearing and objectively reconsider their decisions. If the manager holds his ground in such situations, he will be regarded as stubborn, arrogant, and uncaring. However, if he goes along with a poor suggestion, he, rather than his subordinates, will be held responsible for his poor decision. Due to this disconnect, managers often make decisions based on the facts as they see them, accepting the possibility of negative feelings and resistance from their subordinates as a necessary consequence. Employees respond with feelings of anger and alienation, which nearly always results in decreased efficiency and increased resistance to future decisions.

Managing employee attitudes is critical because the success or failure of decisions depends on their objective merits and on the emotional response of the employees that must implement them. The degree to which those who must execute decisions are willing to accept them plays a key role in the efficiency of the organization. In practice, second-best decisions that are well accepted usually prove more productive than otherwise perfect decisions that are disliked, opposed, and sabotaged. The problem facing managers is how to protect the quality of decisions without compromising the support of their subordinates.[11]

Problems arising from the emotional responses of others are not confined to management-labor relationships within organizations. Informal organizations of managers exist within the formal management structure as well. Consider for example a situation in which Allen, a senior manager, begins a meeting with the middle managers that report to him regarding suggested changes in department operations by announcing his decision to continue with the existing configuration. Almost immediately, arguments ensue, and he finds himself in a conflict with the members of his management team because the changes are perceived as essential

---

11   N. R. F Maier, Allen R. Solem, and Ayesha A. Maier, *Supervisory & Executive Development* (New York: John Wiley & Sons, 1957), 304-305.

to making their jobs easier. Those opposing Allen are likely to feel that his decision is arbitrary and that he has disregarded their views and feelings on the matter.

Allen's decision, however, is neither arbitrary nor based on any inconsiderate view of the needs of the team. His primary motivation in rejecting the suggested changes is the result of an ultimatum issued by the CEO to produce results by the end of the fiscal year or leave the company. Allen has simply decided to play it safe without disclosing this threat because to do so would hurt his pride and diminish his credibility with the members of his team. If they lose confidence in him and leave, or stay and begin to question all of his decisions, his chances of producing the results demanded could be seriously reduced.

Of course, if Allen allows his pride to make him defensive, his team members may sense that something isn't quite right and feel resentment over the fact that he has deliberately concealed information from them about something. This may make them suspicious of his motives and even angrier over what to them appears to be an arbitrary decision against their recommendations. As this occurs, the situation degenerates further into a state of mutual frustration. When this happens, none of those involved is likely to view the disagreements as mere misunderstandings and may be unable to engage in any constructive problem solving.

Allen is faced with two choices: to go it alone and deal with pressures from above and below, or to share the problem with the team in a joint effort to address the situation. To handle this situation successfully, Allen will need to inform the group of his directive from the CEO and ask for their support and ideas in addressing the situation. He can do this without losing credibility if he presents the problem in situational terms in which the entire group is challenged to produce results within the allotted time.

By sharing his problem, Allen dramatically increases his chances of obtaining the team's ideas and support. This will also focus the attention of all concerned on the real problem, which is to show results by the end of the fiscal year or convince the CEO that his directive was ill conceived. The problem will no longer be whether to accept team member suggestions, but simply to determine which of various alternatives will produce the best solution, thus determining how best to respond to the situation.

Allen will need to have confidence in his team members' capability to achieve the goal, and he will need to respect their ideas. When confronted by fear and threats, however, he is not likely to do this, and instead may elect to take the very actions that will increase the likelihood of failure, resistance, and resentment. This is the most typical scenario because most managers have not been trained regarding the fine art of dealing with the informal organizations within their teams and departments. Likewise, most managers find it difficult to share their burdens with their employees.

If Allen had been trained to open channels of communication to address this issue, and if he felt confident in his ability to handle the ensuing discussion, he would have been more likely to share his problem with his team and thereby increase his chances of success.

Allen's reaction to this scenario is typical of most managers in similar situations. Their reactions are based on fear. Fear is more likely to produce avoidance rather than foster the potentially risky collaboration needed to find superior solutions to problems. Avoidance is primarily an emotional reaction and often makes little sense rationally in terms of the facts. Managers who use avoidance as a tactic tend to go it alone and maintain the status quo rather than innovate. Allen is very likely to avoid constructive communication by threatening his subordinates with poor evaluations or termination of employment if their performance does not improve. He may even attempt to avoid dealing with the wisdom of his decisions by ridding himself of employees that disagree with him. Insisting on procedures that have worked in the past is a way to avoid the uncertainty of change. These strategies dramatically increase the likelihood of failure and preempt the possibility of successfully responding to his new circumstances. They are, unfortunately, the norm rather than the exception in American management today.

The idea that there are alternative and new procedures for solving problems sometimes does not occur to managers, and the stress under which they work dramatically decreases the possibility that they will share their burdens with team members and subordinates to increase their chances of success. If managers could learn to act as though they have no real power, the constructive thinking of their teams and the groups they supervise would increase.[12] Of course, the risks associated with this often appear to be overwhelming and drive managers to resort to strategies unlikely to be successful.

Every working group has its own informal organization with its own system of status, values, privileges, and accepted behaviors. When there are changes in procedures that really amount to nothing more than changes in the formal organization, the members of the informal organization within the formal system will inevitably feel threatened. To avoid backlash from subordinates, it is routinely recommended that all changes proposed by management be evaluated in light of their potential social effects within the workplace. This evaluation should be based on an examination of the human needs emphasized within the organization's culture. All needs should be considered, including biological needs for comfort, economic needs for security, social needs for friends, and psychological needs for status and freedom.

In the absence of effective communication processes that allow access to the employees' emotional responses, this is much more easily said than done. Collective needs stem from employees looking to their co-workers to meet their needs for a sense of belonging and for acceptance, and for being listened to and respected. Any of these needs can motivate employees to exhibit conduct that

---

12   Ibid., 319-320.

seems contrary to their self-interest.[13] Furthermore, Conduct that is contrary to the economic interests of employees can only be understood when considered in the social context of the informal organizations within which those employees work.

A failure to consider the power of informal organizations can result in dysfunctional and unwelcome consequences for management, such as generalized belligerence, verbal opposition, and displaced anger. Immature, even childish behavior among employees often results in insubordination and sabotage. Logical explanations fall far short in understanding these responses because employee reactions in such situations stem from unarticulated emotions. Employee logic makes sense only in the context of the values and structure of the social network within which they work. Unfortunately, beyond advocating that managers consider all of the needs of their employees, textbooks dealing with organizational behavior offer very few specific ideas regarding just how these needs can be identified, or how they can be handled once they *are* identified.

The realities of modern business organizations place managers in the position of being unable to control many of the operations for which they are responsible. The old idea that a manager's authority must equal his responsibility is no longer honored in many companies. If a manager lacks confidence in his subordinates or expects antagonism and lack of responsibility on their part, he is placed in a situation that is bound to generate severe stress. Stress usually results in increased reliance on dysfunctional methods of control. Inevitably, the use of heavy-handed attempts to control uncooperative and unsupportive workgroups leads to greater problems and inefficiencies.[14] Increasing reliance on authority, incentives, punishments, and supervision are not the answer. Instead, managers need to improve channels of communication to increase employee cooperation and use the result-

---

13   J. M. Juran, *Managerial Breakthrough*, revised ed. (New York: McGraw-Hill, 1995), 161-163.
14   Douglas McGregor, *The Human Side of Enterprise*, annotated ed., ed. Joel Cutcher-Gershenfeld (New York: McGraw-Hill, 2006), 218-219.

ing trust that engenders to reduce their stress and the tendency to micromanage. Too often, unfortunately, this is more easily said than done. The difficulty in opening communication perpetuates the ongoing problem of strained, inefficient workplace relationships.

Managers' problems actually stem from their education. They tend to gather specialized information regarding a specific industry or skill during their university preparation for their role in a particular industry. Despite their extensive training, they typically enter that industry with little understanding of the difficulties they will encounter if they are to become effective members of an organizational unit. The focus of their education is typically on their specialty and its methods and techniques. The complex problems involved in the effective utilization of this knowledge in the context of working with others has seldom been examined.[15] Many new managers are completely naïve about their professional relationships, about the roles they will play, and the interactions they will encounter when they actually attempt to lead people in the field.

In fact, the training that managers receive often tends to increase their vulnerability to problems originating within the informal organizations associated with the departments or plants they supervise. They have been taught to look for the best solutions to problems without considering the impact of those solutions on the people charged with implementing their directives. They leave their preparatory educational programs with unwarranted confidence in scientific techniques and statistical processes. New managers enter the workplace with the expectation that their subordinates will enthusiastically accept their application of these supposedly proven techniques to find solutions to workplace problems. Management by direction and control seems appropriate to them because their decisions are based on what for them is reli-

---

15   Ibid., 207-208.

able information. They think additional discussion is unwarranted when they have based their decisions on objective facts.

This belief leads managers into the mistaken assumption that no reasonable person would challenge their decisions. They soon find, however, that many of the people with whom they work are not reasonable people—at least not according to the manager's definition. Not only are they not impressed by their managers as people or by their education, they often reject the so-called objective results of their scientific studies and refuse to implement new techniques as directed. It does not take new managers long to decide that many of the people with whom they work are not concerned with the success or failure of the organization for which they work. Instead, they seem to be preoccupied with maintaining their status, quality of life, and satisfaction within the informal organization.

People look to their peers and the social networks within their places of employment for self-esteem, acceptance, and respect. These networks comprise the informal organizations that have evolved within every team, department, and plant. The satisfaction that employees receive from their peers through these networks substantially contributes to the quality of their lives. It is not surprising, therefore, that employees would be preoccupied with maintaining their relationships with their peers in the workplace. These relationships are important to managers as well because high levels of job satisfaction correlate with high self-esteem, self-motivation, efficiency, and positive attitudes toward work.[16]

While it is important to remember that the correlation of these employee characteristics with job satisfaction does not imply a cause-effect relationship, the research definitely shows that these tend to occur together. Studies of employees with high and low self-esteem found that job satisfaction and self-esteem are strongly related. Employees with high job satisfaction tend to have greater

---

16   T. A. Judge, E. A. Locke, C. C. Durham, and A. N. Kluger, "Dispositional effects on job and life satisfaction: The role of core evaluations," *Journal of Applied Psychology* 83, no. 1 (1998): 17-34.

self-esteem than those with lower job satisfaction.[17] Interestingly, the relationship between job satisfaction and other satisfaction doesn't appear to stop with self-esteem. It has been observed that for many people, high levels of job satisfaction are also related to high levels of life satisfaction. This raises the interesting possibility that satisfaction at work may influence satisfaction in other areas of life.[18]

Low levels of job satisfaction have been shown to be related to turnover in an interesting way. While one would expect employees with low job satisfaction to quit their jobs and seek other work, a study published in 1993 revealed a surprising twist with implications for organizational climate. In the study, nurses working in a clinic completed questionnaires regarding their tendency to complain; the study also asked them to indicate how satisfied they were with their jobs. The investigators compared the nurses' job satisfaction with whether or not they eventually quit their jobs at the clinic.

The results of the study indicated that there was no significant relationship between satisfaction and turnover for the nurses who complained frequently. However, for the nurses who complained less, satisfaction was significantly correlated with turnover. This implies that workplaces with social networks that produce little job satisfaction are more likely to retain unhappy people contributing to a negative organizational climate. People with more positive attitudes about life are more likely to find another job when they are unhappy at work.[19] The cost of low job satisfaction can be high, and it can have significant negative consequences for the general climate of a business.

Research also supports the proposition that people who enjoy working with their supervisors and coworkers find more

---

17 G. G. Garske, "The relationship of self-esteem to levels of job satisfaction of vocational rehabilitation professionals," *Journal of Applied Rehabilitation Counseling* 27, no. 2 (1990): 19-22.
18 T. A. Judge and S. Watanabe, "Individual differences in the nature of the relationship between job and life satisfaction," *Journal of Occupational and Organizational Psychology* 67 (1994): 101-107.
19 T. A. Judge, "Does affective disposition moderate the relationship between job satisfaction and voluntary turnover?" *Journal of Applied Psychology* 78 no. 3 (1993): 395-401.

satisfaction at work.[20] When people have coworkers and supervisors who make their jobs unbearable, it is natural that they will be less satisfied than in workplaces where coworkers like and respect one another. In unpleasant work environments, it is only natural that people resent one another and take little ownership of their work. The social network in the workplace has a profound effect on the relationships between coworkers. In supportive environments, coworkers cooperate with one another, which bring high levels of satisfaction for all concerned. In hostile environments, employees are much less efficient because they dislike their workplace. For this reason, managing the social network or informal organization is necessary for a successful company.

In a study of employees working in a manufacturing plant, investigators found that satisfaction with supervisors and coworkers correlated to organizational and team commitment. Greater levels of commitment resulted in greater levels of productivity, lower turnover, and greater cooperation among workers.[21] Social pressures within the workgroup tend to contribute to the well-being of the organization when employees as a group find satisfaction on the job. A positive social pressure develops that sustains employee goodwill. This rarely occurs in the absence of skillful management practices that keep the channels of communication open.

The emotional outcomes of the social interactions among employees can undermine the integrity of teams, departments, and even entire plants if not adequately addressed. Persistent interpersonal problems in the workplace result in lower satisfaction for employees, which brings destructive levels of stress that managers and employees take home to their families. These in turn generate negative emotions and unfortunate responses that

---

20   M. Newsome and V. Pillari, "Job satisfaction and the worker-supervisor, relationship," *The Clinical Supervisor* 9 no. 2 (1992): 119-129. R. L. Repetti and K. A. Cosmas, "The quality of the social environment at work and job satisfaction," *Journal of Applied Social Psychology* 21 no. 10 (1991): 840-854.
21   J. W. Bishop and K. D. Scott, "How commitment affects team performance," *HR Magazine* 42 no. 2 (1997): 107-111.

perpetuate problems that would otherwise dissipate over time. While valuable employees typically leave unsatisfying work environments, dysfunctional employees tend to remain, thus perpetuating the dysfunction.

Unfortunately, there is little practical literature dealing with the interpersonal aspects of the workplace. Books suggesting various manipulative gimmicks are and have always been readily available from the popular press, but they address only the symptoms of dysfunction. Managers who attempt to apply the techniques advocated in these books usually experience mixed success at best and downright embarrassingly public failures at worst. What managers need is a genuine and effective way to work with the people they supervise without resorting to manipulation or power-grabbing schemes.

A review of the classic literature of management that relates to informal organizations is surprisingly helpful. Careful consideration of what has been discovered about these social networks suggests simple but effective processes for improving communication and the interpersonal relations within formal organizations. Consistent use of these techniques will decrease the stress that managers and those who work with them experience, and thereby improve efficiency and morale. The methods advocated in this book are supported in the literature and do not require manipulation or coercion. They have worked very well in completely open settings where what was being done was well understood by everyone involved.

This book explores the foundations underlying interpersonal problems in the workplace and ways to address them through improved communication. The recognition of the importance of interpersonal relations is not new and goes back at least to the advent of scientific management. The discussions of the issues faced by management include the insights of some of the most gifted American managers of the twentieth century. References are provided at the end of the book for those who would like to rediscover the wealth of knowledge, experience, and insight accumulated since the advent of scientific management.

Straightforward communication processes can provide managers with the ability to maintain the support and cooperation of the informal organization of the employees he or she supervises. Improving interpersonal relations, reducing stress, and enlisting the power of cooperation will greatly reduce the complexity faced by managers in furthering the economic objectives of their companies. Communication processes are the key to managing employee social networks

2.

THE INFORMAL ORGANIZATION

The formal organization of a company is its design and operation as conceived by management. Its organizational chart formalizes the intended power structure, the division of responsibilities, channels of communication, and decision-making hierarchies. Workgroups within the company such as teams, departments, and divisions are first delineated by management and later changed as necessary. This formal structure is the product of careful planning based on an economic logic aimed at maximizing profits. It includes the work products of management such as strategic plans, official directives, written policies, accepted practices, routine discipline and reward structures, and communications. It encompasses the design, methods, procedures, and strategies that control the day-to-day operations of the company.

Managers are the formal leaders of the company. They design its formal organization, and then they monitor it, control it, and change its structure as needed. Their efforts in providing direction, supervision, incentives, and punishments are primarily accomplished through planning and communication. The formal organization of every business requires ongoing revision as the company responds to its economic and legal environment. Essentially, the formal organization of every company is created and sustained through the communication skills of its managers.

Managers communicate the instructions and expectations used to coordinate the work of employees through discussions, meetings, actions, and policies. Effective management results in constructive attitudes, productivity, and high morale while ineffective management can undermine and ultimately destroy an organization. Managers are always communicating through facial expressions, body language, and their choice of words regardless of their intent.

It is useful to remember that employees cannot stop listening. Even casual, incidental, and unintended communication can be important. For example, a manager who conveys an unprofessional image through speech or dress, or who wastes employees' time, plays favorites, or is arbitrary sends a message that nearly always contributes to poor morale. Middle- and lower-level managers who relay instructions and information from higher-level managers to their subordinates can contribute to the dysfunction within their company regardless of their intent or the degree to which they are aware of the effects of their actions.

Within every company, division, plant, and department, social networks inevitably evolve among the employees. Chester Barnard was the first to refer to these networks as "informal organizations" to contrast them with the formal organizations of the companies he had observed. Informal organizations are the employee social networks that spring up within every workplace. These informal organizations of employees can further the objectives of companies or thwart even the most elegantly formulated plans of formal management. They consist of the interactions, attitudes, values, pecking orders, opinions, and expectations of coworkers. They develop without conscious planning and are maintained by the employees themselves, not by managers. The leaders of these networks are the employees held in high regard by their peers, and the norms of these groups are maintained through peer pressure.

The structure of informal organizations is based on the relative status of their members as they relate to one another. There is no formal organizational chart, and employees typically have difficulty explaining the organization of their social network. To an impressive extent, informal organizations affect opinions regarding a wide variety of issues such as who should do what, and how workers should react to the policies, procedures, and directives of formal management. The critical importance of informal organizations is that they have incredible power to support or oppose company plans and strategies. Employees will do almost anything to maintain their acceptance and status within the group.

For example, the employees of a department in trouble may hold argumentative coworkers in high regard, and expect members of their group to resist the manager informally, by ignoring him or her, and formally, by frequently filing grievances. Resistance often manifests itself in the decision of employees to engage in minor violations of company policies and do the minimal amount of work that is absolutely required to keep their jobs. Employees who refuse to observe the norms set by their social networks are punished in a variety of ways, and if they don't comply, transfer, or resign, they will ultimately be isolated, shunned, and ignored by their coworkers.

The high-status employees are the leaders of the informal organization and they maintain discipline through friendships, gossip, practical jokes, sabotage, and even overt force. High-status employees exert their influence through peer pressure. Showing respect to peers by conversing and eating with them exerts a powerful influence on the attitudes and opinions of every member of the social network. Employees who don't fall in line may be shunned or targeted for practical jokes, ridicule, and even violence.

For example, employees tease peers who dress differently, disagree with higher-status peers, or work harder than sanctioned by the informal organization. The informal organization can be even more important to its members than the company itself. Managers who lack the skill to deal with informal organizations are rarely successful in maximizing the potential of their departments and plants. Due to the way these social networks develop, informal organizations can produce negative effects on workers that go far beyond the workplace. Employees trapped within dysfunctional informal organizations suffer at home as well as at work.

Group pressure for conformity to the unspoken policies of the informal organization usually increases at first and then gradually decreases as the group isolates those members who don't conform. For a time, the typical nonconforming coworker will experience increasing peer pressure from coworkers in the form of "friendly" reminders, sarcasm, practical jokes, sabotage, and shunning. If they don't withdraw from the group by quitting or transferring, nonconformists are ultimately ostracized and ignored. Few employees can tolerate working in social isolation.

For example, a highly productive employee will often begin to produce less, transfer to a different department, or become a loner after being in a group that does not approve of his or her efficiency. In such situations, the total productivity of the group remains unaffected. By the same token, it is well known that new members of a group and existing members who suffer from low status or isolation may increase their status and acceptance within their groups by conforming to group norms. As their status improves, they will enjoy increasingly positive relationships with their coworkers. For example, if members of a group eat lunch together, a new member can improve his or her status by joining them for lunch. If coworkers wear ties, a new employee should wear a tie as well.

It is common for a new member of a group to be unaware of why she is being hazed by coworkers. Although she may be acutely aware of their mistreatment and lack of acceptance, she may not know what she needs to change to gain acceptance, or even how to change. While coworkers can be quite unambiguous in indicating disapproval, they're not always clear regarding what it is that is offending them. New employees may fail to take them seriously or react with stubbornness and anger. Nevertheless, the hostile behavior of coworkers usually diminishes when new employees "learn their place," "know the score," or "get in line."

The identification of the informal leaders in an organization presents some unique challenges. They are not identifiable by title and function, and they do not appear on any organizational chart. They may not even be conscious of the leadership roles they play. Their informal leadership is not the result of planning, nor is it aimed at attaining long-term goals. In fact, informal employee leaders are typically motivated by emotional rather than rational aims. They enjoy having power, and they enjoy the attention they receive while exercising their power in conflict with other employees or managers.

Nevertheless, managers who understand differentiation within groups can reliably identify the informal leaders among their employees. Essentially, the power of employee leaders stems from their higher status within their groups, and they are motivated by a desire to maintain or increase their power. The fact that this motivation can be stronger even than monetary rewards and formal recognition goes far in explaining why overt attempts by managers to motivate employees through punishments, incentives, and formal recognition are often unfruitful.

In the early 1900s, Frederick Winslow Taylor attributed soldiering, or working below capacity, to the natural laziness of human beings. Although the decision of an individual worker to soldier could be ignored, systematic soldiering—groups of employees working below capacity—has far more important implications for managers. Taylor noted that systematic soldiering was an almost universal phenomenon present in nearly every organization utilizing typical systems of management. Although he was unaware of what would come to be known as the informal organization, he was convinced that systematic soldiering resulted from the belief of the employees as a group that working below capacity would promote their joint interests. In short, he had observed the informal organizations that evolve within all companies.

Taylor gave an example of the peer pressures exerted by members of an informal organization of golf caddies that promoted soldiering. He related the story of a twelve-year-old experienced golf caddy explaining to a new caddy that had shown unusual energy that caddies should move slowly and lag behind when their golfers walked to their balls. Since caddies were paid by the hour, the faster they walked the less money they earned. To make certain that he would be taken seriously, the experienced caddy finished his advice by telling the inexperienced caddy that if he continued to walk too fast, the other boys would beat him up. This is a prime example of how soldiering is induced and enforced by an existing informal organization of employees.[22]

This was one of the first observations of informal organizations opposing efficiency. Systematic soldiering is widespread due to the influence of informal organizations that tend to make it in each worker's interest to avoid doing any job faster or better than it has been done in the past. Taylor ascribed this phenomenon to misapplication of incentives by management and mistrust of incentives by workers, but this is actually rarely the case. While inept application of incentives by management can take many forms, the mistrust of workers usually arises from the practice of management reducing wages to previous levels with heightened expectations after incentives have produced improvements in productivity.

In the situation involving the golf caddies, the response of the informal organization to the risk of having their wages reduced was to educate new caddies as they joined the group and punish experienced caddies for any sort of rate busting. This principle is active today in virtually every industry. As new workers join formally organized departments, gangs, or teams, the experienced workers will tend to use whatever verbal persuasion and social pressure is necessary to stop the new recruits from temporarily increasing their wages at the long-term expense of the group. Informal organizations of employees have the power to neutralize any incentive program designed by management.

---

22   Taylor, *The Principles of Scientific Management*, 11-12.

Systematic soldiering is especially likely to develop in situations where workers perform piecework in which their pay is determined by how many pieces they produce in a given time. Once a worker's price per piece is reduced after having worked harder to increase his output under an incentive plan, he is likely to become angry with his employer. This underlying anger results in distrust of incentive programs and a determination to avoid future cuts by soldiering.

Workers who fear for their interests feel justified in intentionally misleading and deceiving their employers. The fear is that as soon as productivity has increased, the minimum requirements of workers will be increased and the incentives will be withdrawn. This results in workers being required to work harder for the same rate of pay.[23] The primary force behind this reaction of the informal organization is fear. How to deal with the fears of the informal organization is a problem that managers have universally found frustrating and difficult to address. Nevertheless, it is clear that systematic soldiering results from the influence of the informal organizations of workers within companies.

In the absence of the support of the informal organizations of employees, incentive plans produce short-term gains in productivity at the expense of worker integrity. Workers come to view their employers' interests as antagonistic and inconsistent with their own. The mutual confidence that should exist between employers and employees deteriorates, and the feeling that they share in the results of their labor is destroyed. In addition, fear, mistrust, antagonism, and lack of enthusiasm are the inevitable byproducts of mismanaged and poorly managed informal organizations, all of which will severely handicap the functioning of any business.[24]

Negative sentiments strike right at the heart of the functioning of every formal organization. The principal asset or treasure

---

23   Ibid., 13.
24   Ibid., 14.

of any group, if you will, is the accumulated mass of knowledge regarding the specific tasks done by members of the group. This is particularly true of the trades, and experienced managers recognize the fact that the people they supervise—the ones who are actually doing the work—possess more of this knowledge than any individual manager or team of managers. Performing a given set of tasks daily for a very long period imparts a level of experience that cannot be acquired in any other way.

Even exceptionally successful workers who become managers are aware of the fact that their own knowledge and skills fall far short of the combined knowledge and skill of all of the workers they supervise. Frederick Winslow Taylor noted that the best managers often turned the problem of doing the work in the most efficient and economical way over to their subordinates. Managers have long recognized the value of skilled employees working within a social network that is supportive of them, and every experienced manager is aware of the risks presented by angry employees who set out to teach the boss a lesson simply by doing exactly what they are told even when they know their manager has made a mistake.

The task of managers is to induce those they supervise to use their best knowledge, skill, work, effort, and ingenuity while completing the tasks assigned to them. To accomplish this, the employees' good will is indispensible. To obtain the greatest contribution from employees, managers must enlist their initiative, creativity, and support. Unfortunately, this is precisely what dysfunctional, informal employee organizations suppress.[25] Very few employees will dare to support or assist their managers when their peers punish them for cooperating with the boss.

So just how widespread is the dysfunction of informal organizations? Taylor estimated the problem to exist in 90 percent of the industrial organizations he studied. He noted that workers believed it to be directly against their best interests to give their

25   Taylor, *The Principles of Scientific Management*, 23.

employers their best initiative. Instead of utilizing their specialized knowledge, skill, and experience to improve efficiency and productivity, they deliberately soldiered while attempting to deceive their managers by making them believe that they were working as fast as possible.[26]

The best management practices in ordinary use in Taylor's time were those in which workers motivated by skillfully designed incentives gave managers their best initiative. He called this management by initiative and incentive and distinguished it from the scientific management he advocated. Unfortunately, employers have a strong tendency to dilute incentives after productivity increases, and employees who are well aware that they may eventually be required to work harder for the same pay (or even less pay) often react with fear and anger. For these reasons, management by initiative and incentive was not ideal, and Taylor sought to improve on it. He believed that scientific observation could improve on the knowledge of both employees and managers, and that every industry could implement sustainable incentives.[27] Although Taylor correctly identified the problem, scientific management did not successfully address the question of how to deal with informal organizations.

Experience demonstrates that when people are grouped together in gangs, departments, or teams, each person often becomes less efficient than when working alone. In group environments, the productivity and efficiency of otherwise highly motivated workers usually decreases to the level of the least efficient high-status employees in the group. Only very rarely does the introduction of highly efficient employees result in an increase in the productivity of other individuals in the group or of the group as a whole. It is nearly impossible to increase efficiency in the absence of a well-managed informal organization that promotes the interests of the company.

---

26   Ibid., 24.
27   Ibid., 25.

Taylor reported that this phenomenon was the reason behind an order issued by the general superintendent of the Bethlehem Steel Works prohibiting more than four men to a labor gang without specific permission. Whenever possible, each worker was given separate tasks.[28] This strategy was an early attempt to frustrate the informal organization at the steel works through the physical isolation of its members. While management acknowledged the existence of the power of the social network, it was not successful in dissolving the informal organization that had evolved at the plant. The problem of managing informal organizations cannot be side-stepped simply by isolating workers through grouping.

In another interesting story from the Bethlehem Steel Works related by Taylor, some workers who had proved to be very efficient and productive were offered more compensation for their work by another company. The men left the Bethlehem plant in which the informal organization was supportive of management to accept the higher rate. When they announced that they had decided to change companies, the Bethlehem management told the workers that they were sorry to lose them, and assured them that they could always come back to work at Bethlehem Steel if things didn't work out. Within six weeks, nearly all of the workers had returned to Bethlehem because the informal organization of the other company did not accept them.

The men who returned reported that they were not able to earn as much money at the company offering more compensation as they could at Bethlehem because of pressure from the workers they encountered there. Upon arrival at the new company, they were placed with other men who were existing employees, not other new employees. When the new workers began to do their jobs in the same way as they had done them at Bethlehem, they ran into opposition from these employees. The informal organization's lack of tolerance for the new company's incentive plan made it impossible for the workers to participate. The social network at

---

28   Ibid., 60-61.

the company effectively nullified the effectiveness of the company's incentive plan. Not only did the plan fail to increase productivity, but it actually encouraged existing employees to drive away the new, highly efficient employees.

When one of the workers who returned to Bethlehem Steel was asked why he had left the higher-paying job at the other plant, he related the following experience. When he noticed that a certain man who was doing very little work on the job, he asked him why he wasn't working, and he commented that they would not be paid if they didn't do the work. The man who wasn't working asked him who he thought he was and told him to mind his own business. The other established coworkers promptly backed him up and made it clear that they would resort to violence if the Bethlehem men continued to work too quickly. In this instance, members of the informal organization were willing to escalate peer pressure to violence rather than allow outsiders to participate in management's incentive program. Ultimately, the men from Bethlehem made peace by working as slowly as the men in the gang worked. This resulted in their earning less than what they had earned at Bethlehem in spite of the higher rates of compensation.[29]

Peer pressure can be a critical factor in the effectiveness of even the most carefully designed incentive plans. This goes far to explain why the same incentive program can be successful in one department but not in another within the same company. At a minimum, programs designed to increase productivity require the tolerance of the employees' social network.

The power of informal organizations is not limited merely to nullifying incentive plans, but it can actually inspire workers to make decisions that are not in their own best interest. Frederick Winslow Taylor recounted a personally frustrating encounter with the informal organization operating in a factory when he attempted to reduce the workday for female ball bearing inspectors from 10.5 to 8.5 hours without reducing their pay for a shorter

---

29 Taylor, *The Principles of Scientific Management*, 63-64.

day's work. In a relatively rare attempt to improve his reputation for tact, Taylor decided to allow the workers to vote on whether or not their workday would be reduced without any reduction in wages whatsoever.

The economic logic of the proposal was clear. It was in the best interest of the employees to agree to fewer hours because they would be paid more for the hours they worked and have more free time. Amazingly, the employees unanimously voted to maintain the 10.5-hour workday even though their pay would stay the same. Eventually, the company reduced the length of the workday in successive steps without employee input. Interestingly, employee output increased with each successive shortening of the day.[30] Taylor was startled by the apparently absurd behavior of the employees when they were given an opportunity to vote.

This is a clear example of the power of the informal organization at work. The power of the employee social network was sufficient to move the employees to unanimously vote against their economic best interest. Such a result is evidence that the decisions made by informal organizations are not rational in the same way that management decisions are. Making sense of employee behavior that is not based on economic logic is very difficult for managers. The social logic of informal organizations is emotionally based. This goes far in explaining why managers, even managers of genius such as Frederick Winslow Taylor, find their attempts to manage informal organizations confusing and frustrating. When the collective goals and values of the employees are not consistent with the company's objectives, economic incentives are powerless.

As early as the advent of scientific management, Taylor sought an explanation for such apparently irrational behavior in the underlying weakness of management. When managers attempt to solve employee problems alone, they find themselves at a disadvantage. Once managers take on the burden of problem solving, they place employees in a position to find fault with the solutions

---

30   Ibid., 75.

and to choose to facilitate or sabotage the efforts to solve the problem.[31] The answer, however, is not simply turning problems over to employees in the absence of management either. Although employees who have solved their own problems do not oppose the solutions, their solutions vary widely in effectiveness and practicality. Their priorities are only rarely those of management. Instead, Taylor advocated management's use of the scientific method to identify optimum solutions and the skillful application of sustainable incentives and differential pay to induce employees to cooperate.

Nearly identical strategies and actions on the part of management produce beneficial results in one situation and disastrous problems in another.[32] Taylor recognized that many managers mistakenly attributed their personal failures in working effectively with their employees to defects in the principles of scientific management. This was not the case. What unsuccessful managers were actually experiencing was the differential reactions of unmanaged informal organizations to their directives. Taylor realized that even in situations where managers who thoroughly agreed with the principles of scientific management attempted to implement changes too rapidly, they encountered serious difficulties, strikes, and ultimately failure.[33]

Rapid change is almost impossible without the support of the employee social network. In an effort to address the problems created by the informal organizations of employees, Taylor advocated a "complete revolution in the mental attitude and habits" of both workers and managers. He thought this change in attitude could be brought about only through significant education and experience. The idea was that both groups could be convinced of the superiority of the newer methods and recommendations of management and consultants. He was certain that if employees under-

---

31 Taylor, *The Principles of Scientific Management*, 89.
32 Ibid., 112.
33 Ibid., 114.

stood the economic logic behind the policies of management, they would support the implementation of scientific management.

This process would of course require a significant length of time before changes in attitudes could be realistically expected. Based on his extensive experience, Taylor estimated the time required would range from two to five years depending on the complexity of the organizations and the nature of the changes being implemented.[34] Unfortunately, he was unable to revolutionize the attitudes of either employees or managers, and the history of scientific management is full of controversy and opposition. The chief problem Taylor never solved was how to manage informal organizations. He never fully understood that the attitudes of employees are not founded on the economic logic of management.

In the 1930s, Elton Mayo was engaged by the Western Electric Company to assess the effect of illumination on the productivity of factory workers.[35] In the course of his now famous research, Mayo learned that companies employing thousands of workers tend to develop their own solutions to problems in the workplace. These solutions manifest themselves in company methods, policies, and procedures. This characteristic of large companies was responsible for a great many variables that were difficult to control and presented challenges to the generalization of experimental results.

Due to the case-by-case development of institutionalized responses to problems in the workplace, companies lacked satisfactory criteria for the systematic evaluation of management's effectiveness in dealing with people.[36] Mayo's approach to this problem was to study workers' reactions to various managerial interventions with careful attention being paid to the neutralization of extraneous variables. Various factors affecting workers were manipulated experimentally, and the responses of the workers were observed and compared with those of control groups. Mayo hoped that

---

34 Ibid., 34.
35 Elton Mayo, *The Human Problems of an Industrial Civilization*, 2nd ed. (Cambridge: Division of Research, Graduate School of Business Administration, Harvard University, 1946), 55.
36 Ibid., 56.

effective variables could be isolated sufficiently to apply his findings to other workplaces.

The major discovery coming from the experiments conducted at the Hawthorne plant was the realization that something was at work besides the variables being manipulated. It became clear to Mayo's research group that the changes in variables only accounted for minor differences from one period to another and between the experimental groups and control groups.[37] The controls in his research revealed that researchers had overlooked a very powerful variable: the informal organization. His group was observing the effects of that variable, which had a far greater impact on employee productivity, attitudes, and behavior than any of the variables they were manipulating within the experimental groups.

The research group had discovered that notwithstanding changes in the variables, production continued to increase due to the support of the informal organization of employees participating in the study. Mayo's group suspected that this effect was caused by the research process itself, simply because the researchers interacted with the employees. The effect was subsequently well documented and came to be known as the Hawthorne Effect. Today, experimental designs in human resources that fail to control for this effect are usually considered defective.

So, just how powerful was the effect generated by the informal organization at the Hawthorne Plant? Mayo indicated that production increased during his experiments from an average weekly output of approximately 2,400 relays per operator to approximately 3,000 relays—nearly 25 percent![38] This increase in productivity took place despite the withdrawal of incentive and privileges, and the effects were relatively permanent and did not respond to other changes in variables that resulted in decreased efficiency in other departments. But why did the interaction of researchers with workers in the test groups generate this effect?

---

37   Ibid., 65.
38   Elton Mayo, *The Human Problems of an Industrial Civilization*, 2nd ed. (Cambridge: Division of Research, Graduate School of Business Administration, Harvard University, 1946), 66.

Mayo focused on the psychological aspects of the interaction between employees and researchers. He found that the communication between managers and their subordinates itself seemed to be responsible. Because informal organizations are emotionally rather than rationally based, the very act of speaking with employees can have a greater impact on their attitudes than the rational content of the communications themselves. This is consistent with the common experience most people have of feeling better after discussing a problem even though no solution has been or can be identified.

Mayo had stumbled upon the key to managing employee attitudes. Skillful communication is effective in managing informal organizations and securing their support for company objectives.

When Mayo's group questioned workers in an attempt to learn why production had increased in the test room, they learned that the interactions between the researchers and workers generated durable affective responses. Workers reported that they felt that their working conditions were "pleasanter, freer, and happier" than they were prior to the experiment. It was concluded that production could possibly be increased throughout the industry by management's having more personal considerations for workers regardless of their level of employment.[39] However, the research group did not recommend any specific techniques for doing that.

Mayo was convinced that payment incentives and higher earnings played only a minor role in determining the productivity of workers at that plant. He attributed the major role to changes in the mental attitude of the workers themselves. In addition, a sympathetic and interested chief observer managed the test room. He avoided behaving in the manner of most supervisors because he did not want to compromise the study. This meant that he did not assume the mantle of "the boss."[40] This had the psychological effect of enabling workers to achieve a mental steady state, which

---

39   Ibid., 69.
40   Ibid., 70-71.

was highly resistant to changes in external conditions such as the systematic manipulation of the other variables being studied.

He hinted at the existence of the informal organization by stating that the Western Electric experiments affected the informal organization of the workers themselves by strengthening their inner equilibrium, which he freely described as temperamental.[41]

The effects generated by employee social networks are powerful, and they bring stability to the work environment. If managers can enlist the assistance of informal organizations in pursuing company objectives, workers will remain productive and even increase production in periods of adverse conditions affecting both themselves and their companies. The power of the informal organization at the Hawthorne plant was astounding and previously untapped.

The performance of the workers in the department continually improved nearly unaffected by the changes in the experimental conditions manipulated by the investigators. The increasing productivity was accompanied by marked improvements in employee attitudes toward their work, their managers, and the company. Simply speaking to employees at Hawthorne had an effect powerful enough to swamp the influence of the variables that were the subject of the research. The informal organization was present and supportive in response to the researchers' communication with employees.

Mayo's researchers concluded that employee attitudes and performance were directly correlated. It was more likely that improved morale had increased efficiency than any other variable manipulated in the experiments. The group had discovered that modifications in managerial communication were capable of having a significantly impact on generally held attitudes and opinions among employees. Mayo's researchers had identified a powerful tool capable of managing informal organizations.

In explaining more fully the specific situation in the test room, one of the investigators indicated that the relationships between the supervisor and the workers had improved to the extent that

---

41   Mayo, *The Human Problems of an Industrial Civilization*, p. 75.

supervision was almost unnecessary. The supervisor felt such confidence and friendliness toward workers that he was comfortable relying on them to do their very best. This is typical of the emotional response of managers working with supportive informal organizations. Appropriate communication with employees reduces stress for managers as well as for those they supervise.

In reporting their own emotional reactions to this communication, the workers indicated that they had no sensation of working more quickly. Rather, they indicated that they experienced less tension under the experimental conditions than under those prevailing prior to the research. They did not regard their supervisor as "the boss" and felt happier.[42] Workers actually reported feeling better about their work environments, their supervisors, and their work while working more quickly. They did not feel they were working harder despite their increased productivity. A contented informal organization freed employees to work more to their capacity without stressing them.

Although Mayo first experienced the power of informal organizations, he did not fully understand the nature of employee social networks or how they operated. Insight into what exactly an informal organization is was first offered by Chester Barnard in the 1940s. Barnard conceived of groups of employees as units with which their members interact. These groups are social in the sense that they are not merely the sum of the interactions of the individuals within them. There is something more. Social groups present systems of social interaction in addition to the individual interactions of their members. In other words, groups interact with their individual members as a unique entity.

Interactions arising from group relationships operate on the personal psychology of the people comprising the group. This is consistent with Mayo's observations at the Hawthorne plant. A group itself can induce psychological changes in its members in terms of attitude, motivation, and action that would not otherwise

---

42   Ibid., 77-78.

take place. When these changes in attitudes and opinions are compatible with the objectives and activities of the company, employees are efficient and have high morale. Employees who feel that they are appreciated and that their work is important focus on doing their jobs as well as they can even in adverse conditions. The objectives of their companies become their personal objectives.

The willingness of employees to cooperate with management is largely affected by the informal organization to which they belong. When employee social networks are supportive of their companies' objectives, employees work more efficiently and tend to work with managers to address counterproductive situations.[43] Similarly, when informal organizations are not cooperative due to unwilling employees who are unconcerned about company objectives, the effectiveness and viability of the company itself is hindered. While the management literature acknowledges this, there have been few efforts to document the costs and savings associated with varying levels of support within companies. This is largely because so little is known regarding the communication processes capable of increasing the support of informal organizations.

The processes of informal organizations are for the most part unconscious and emotionally driven while those of formal organizations are conscious, planned, goal directed and rational. Notwithstanding this, they play a critical role in establishing reality for employees in the workplace. The unconscious processes of employees' social networks give rise to customs, habits and expectations that have a profound impact on nearly every formal undertaking of the companies in which they exist.[44]

Interestingly, these processes are extremely resistant to direct attempts to intervene on the part of management. While the formal and informal organizations of companies are independent of one another, they are at the same time interdependent. Barnard asserted that one cannot exist without the other. The failure

---

43   Barnard, *The Functions of the Executive*, 41-42
44   Ibid., 116.

of either one results in the disintegration of the other.[45] If the company fails, the employees lose their jobs and their informal organization within the company dissolves. If the informal organization of employees falls apart, employees cannot cooperate or work together, and the company will go out of business.

Formal organizations are the product of planning for concerted effort toward definite objectives. In business, they are consciously planned before employees are ever recruited to work in them. In this sense, they are prior in time and essential to the evolution of their associated informal organizations. However, once employees are hired and begin to work in groups, informal organizations evolve of necessity from the daily interactions of those employees as coworkers. The growth of informal organizations is inevitable because most employee interactions within the formal subdivisions of companies are not governed by the policies and directives of management. Cooperation is informal and dependent on the attitudes, personalities, and practices of the individuals working together.

Barnard noted that even highly experienced managers tend to deny or at least neglect the existence of informal organizations within their companies. Most executives are unaware of the influence of informal organizations on employees despite the fact that they have such a commanding influence on employees' morale, motivation, and effectiveness.[46] Whether this lack of awareness is due to the pressures of work or to a reluctance to acknowledge the existence of an employee social network that operates unconsciously, irrationally, and independently of the formal structure of the company is still to be determined. Regardless of the reason for it, Barnard believed this lack of awareness is not confined to businesses, but extends to all formal groups including political, educational, religious, and military organizations.

---

45   Ibid., 120.
46   Barnard, *The Functions of the Executive*, 120-122.

Ironically, this lack of direct awareness is belied by the fact that everyone who has had the experience of working with other people knows the first task on taking a new job is to learn the unwritten rules of the workplace. This amounts to learning who's who and understanding the customs, values, and expectations of the informal society within the workgroup (the informal organization). This task is not undertaken by a thorough study of any of the work products of management such as company policies, strategic plans, and directives. Learning to fit in is indispensible to every employee, and the task is undertaken immediately on accepting employment. Failing to earn a place in the informal organization has serious consequences for new employees.

Studying the formal work products of management to learn how to function in a specific workgroup is rather like learning how to drive simply by reading statutes, court decisions, and books about driving without ever taking a vehicle out on the road. The information is useful and perhaps even indispensible, but without the personal experience acquired by encountering other drivers on the road, accidents are to be expected. Without personal interactions with the individuals comprising the workgroup, new employees can expect a rough go until they become familiar enough with the existing social network to be accepted by the group. This adds to the stress involved in starting a new job and very often drives highly competent employees away.

A few of the functions of informal organizations within companies are the maintenance of cohesiveness, morale, and order. The informal processes at work among employees heavily influence their willingness to serve the objectives of the company and honor the authority of their managers. The efficiency of communication is enhanced thorough the reduction of the need for formal managerial decisions on relatively minor aspects of the work of the group and the interactions of the employees involved.[47] They are

---

47   Barnard, *The Functions of the Executive*, 227.

also largely responsible for inculcating feelings of personal integrity, self-respect, and independence among employees.

Since the interactions within employee social networks are not conscious or planned, managers typically find them difficult to understand and almost impossible to manage. Informal employee groups are not directed by managers and are not focused on the impersonal objectives of the company, as are managers. Interactions within informal organizations are characterized by the differential reinforcement of choices made and attitudes expressed by employees and their peers. Informal organizations may provide employees with a means of maintaining their individuality in formal working environments, which tend to depersonalize interactions through emphasis on group objectives.[48]

The formal structures of companies are summarized in organizational charts. These structures are hierarchical in the sense that positions within companies vary in importance, power, and responsibility. Managers understand that problems will arise anytime the established hierarchy is overlooked in the decision-making process. Each position carries a differing status based on its relative position within the formal hierarchy. Authority is conferred to managers by the jobs they hold, their title, and to whom they report. Status differences within management are formalized in writing and are well understood by employees and managers alike.

However, this is not usually the case with regard to status differences among employees. To be successful, a manager must have at least a limited understanding of status differences among the employees her or she supervises. When status differences are related to the formal organization of the workgroup, they are more easily accepted by managers. For example, a supervisor may be aware that mechanics will ask their assistants to go out for coffee, but assistants cannot expect mechanics to take a turn. In this situation, the status differences arise from the fact that mechanics are paid more and their jobs are considered more prestigious

---

48   Ibid., 122.

than the assistants' jobs are. Consequently, most supervisors in this situation would expect problems to arise if an assistant rebelled by refusing to go for coffee.

However, when status differences are related to other factors such as employee preferences, prejudices, and emotions, managers find it very difficult to accept them and may even attempt to ignore them. Most supervisors have even less understanding when a problem based on status involves jobs in which the pay rates and job grades are nearly equal, such as where status is more exclusively the product of the informal organization than economic considerations or the company's organizational chart. This can result in poor decisions with negative consequences that mystify managers leaving them frustrated, suspicious, and angry over employee reactions.

For example, a warehouse manager moved an order picker to a dock position and encountered a variety of unexpected reactions by his subordinates. The order picker hesitated, and the other dockworkers openly complained that they didn't understand the move. A number of angry merchandise packers began to talk about a walkout. Although the pay scales within the workgroup were relatively equal and the various positions mentioned occupied approximately the same level on the company's organizational chart, the informal organization had given these positions different status levels. Within the employee social network, the ascending order of these jobs was as follows: order picker, assistant merchandise packer, lead merchandise packer, and dockworker. To give a picker a dock job before "he had paid his dues" was arbitrary and unreasonable in the minds of the men in the warehouse.

In this situation, what the manager thought of as a single group of people had been divided into four classes within the informal organization. This division was the source of the social status issue. Because the group had been split into four factions, the issue did not focus on the same problem that the supervisor had addressed. Instead, it degenerated into a struggle over the perceived status of the employees involved and produced a great deal of dysfunctional behavior on the part of the employees involved. Until the struggle between the supervisor and the employees could be resolved, reduced cooperation and perceptions of a lack of fairness would persist and continue to generate new and seemingly unrelated problems for management.

Status within informal organizations is an important nonfinancial motivator for members of every employee group. Many jobs acquire low status because they are routine, dirty, and simple, and because they are performed by low status employees. Jobs performed by senior workers can acquire high status simply because the workers performing them are viewed as somehow superior to other workers.[49] While managers may be unaware of these subtleties, employees are acutely aware of them. The economic incentives controlled by management are no match for the nonfinancial motivators controlled by employee social networks. In other words, jobs can acquire varying levels of status due to the nature of the job and the characteristics of the employees performing them. Once the job has acquired a certain status, employees taking the job are given the status of the job within the informal organization.

It is common for the informal organization within a relatively homogeneous group to go unnoticed by the supervisor of the group. In fact, even members of the group may be unaware of the informal organization in which they work until someone or some event disturbs the status quo. Norman Maier, the father of group-in-action training for managers, which was popular in the 1950s, noted that the tendency for an informal social structure to develop was so strong that it occurred even among groups of animals. For instance, chickens develop a pecking order almost as soon as they're placed together in the coop.[50] It is sobering to note that employees develop a "pecking order" in every company.

---

49   Maier, Solem, and Maier, *Supervisory & Executive Development*, 192.
50   Ibid., 49-50.

Social structuring develops within all companies regardless of their size. Its presence leads to misunderstanding and frustration when it interferes with management's directives. Maier thought that these informal organizations might arise because they satisfied needs of their members and protected to some extent the rights to a degree of freedom within the workplace. Others ascribe the cause of these organizations to the requirements of communication within the employee groups themselves. Regardless of the underlying causes, informal employee organizations arise out of the differing preferences of their members. Popularity, seniority, ethnicity, education, skill, and physical appearance can affect interpersonal relations to the point that these factors become part of the informal organization operating within a company and escape the attention of even the most dedicated supervisor.

Fluctuations in the market, changes in the competitive environment, or advances in engineering may require a business to make changes in equipment, operations, and production methods. Any change naturally involves the entire organization in problem solving. New patterns of consumer behavior must be anticipated, the introduction of new equipment and the adaptation of existing facilities must be coordinated, job description and compensation rates may need to be altered, and employees may require additional training. Management is typically very capable in developing satisfactory and even ingenious solutions to these problems through the planning and supervisory functions of the formal organization of the company.

However, the implementation of management's solutions to problems is based on economic logic. Furthermore, implementation can seldom be confined to the technical aspects of company operations. The solutions to problems fashioned by management are the products of planning, and as such, they inevitably entail alterations in the work of the employees. Although new methods may be fair, high quality, workable, and efficient from an objective standpoint, they will not be successful if they are not acceptable to the informal organization of employees concerned, and this organization does not operate exclusively on economic logic.

Maier noted that the necessity of employee acceptance makes solving the problems resulting from change within an organization much different from the purely technical problem of evaluating new equipment or designing new procedures. When he wrote about this in the 1950s, he noted that the concern of management with employee acceptance of solutions to problems developed by management was at that time still only a very recent development. The quality and acceptability of solutions to problems are very different characteristics that are independent of one another to a certain degree. Management has control over the quality of solutions to problems because it develops them itself. However, acceptance of the changes in work entailed by those solutions is not within the control of management.

Acceptance is voluntary on the part of employees and profoundly influenced by the informal organization operating within the workgroup. It is not subject to the will of management or directly controlled by incentive, directive, policy, or authority. Opposition may be direct or indirect. For example, the lack of acceptance is often expressed through grievances, resignations, slowdowns, and hostility toward management. In some instances, employee dissatisfaction is displayed through increased waste, poor workmanship, return to old methods in the absence of direct supervision, excessive absenteeism, and even sabotage.

According to Maier, concerns with employees' negative reactions to change have led to the development of a variety of strategies for dealing with them.[51] One method that has evolved is the selling approach, which largely involves attempting to sell the employees on the need and usefulness of the solutions developed by management prior to any attempted implementation. The selling process involves informing employees of the facts as perceived by management and making arguments in favor of the implemen-

---

51   Ibid., 82-84.

tation of the solutions developed. This strategy is based on the assumption that if employees have the same information as management they will arrive at the same solutions to the problems being addressed.

Unfortunately, the assumption that the informal organization is directly responsive to management's economic logic is not correct. Employee resistance is only rarely based on a lack of information or the structure of financial incentives. The informal organization operating within employee workgroups focuses on the self-actualizing needs of employees. Lack of acceptance by employees typically involves insecurity, distrust, envy, anxiety, acceptance, respect, and status. Facts, numbers, and logic do not go far in meeting the needs of employees responding to emotional concerns. They have little effect on changing negative employee attitudes. Consequently, the selling approach generally has relatively little success and often results in the further polarization of employees and management.

Another strategy for making management's decisions more acceptable is the consultation approach in which management involves employees by consulting with them regarding company problems and considering their contribution prior to adopting solutions. Managers using this approach present the facts to their employees and invite them to share their ideas and feelings while reserving the right to accept or reject their contributions as management sees fit. This approach is generally more successful than the selling approach because it invites the expression of employee opinions while the selling approach simply calls for the adoption of management's point of view.

Managers feel that as long as management reserves the right to accept or reject the employee input into the decision, the quality of the decision is protected. Unfortunately, employees often find management's decisions even more objectionable than they would have under the selling approach when their contributions need to be rejected because they do not conform to the company's economic logic. One way around this has been for management to agree to honor employee opinions and suggestions, but this raises serious issues regarding the relative importance of a solution's quality and economic viability versus its acceptability. Is quality or acceptability of paramount importance? These two factors are so critical to the success of solutions to problems in the workplace that it is often almost impossible to choose one as being more important than the other. Consequently, the consultation approach is also seriously flawed.

Maier took the position that there may well be no single best approach to dealing with the acceptability issues when management introduces change in the workplace. Any suggestion of change in response to a problem automatically elicits a complex series of employee reactions. Managers who are unaware of this often respond in ways that actually compound the problems they are trying to address. Each employee reacts in a different way and to a different degree than the others in the workgroup. They share their reactions with one another, and their combined reactions become that of the informal organization.

Employees may question what effect the proposed changes may have on their compensation, their future chances for promotion, and their status, respect, and acceptance within the workgroup. Proposed changes bring employees face to face with the unknown on many levels. Their reactions are also greatly influenced by the reactions of their peers as a group both in terms of behavior and attitudes. Resistance to change is influenced by a variety of factors because change threatens important employee interests. Managers who believe they can make changes without threatening employee interests by discussing issues objectively do not understand their subordinates or the operations of their informal organizations. The key to managing change lies in effectively managing the social networks of employees—their informal organizations.

3.

THE ROOTS OF DISCONTENT

Informal organizations evolve within all organizations and profoundly influence their effectiveness. They're often difficult for managers to observe and frustrating to encounter because they're not governed by the economic logic of management and therefore are not considered in most planning processes. However, their presence cannot be ignored in today's global economy. Unmanaged informal organizations almost never contribute to the productivity or efficiency of the companies in which they exist.

The reason for this is that unmanaged informal organizations are generally neutral or at least slightly negative toward management in stable environments. In the absence of change, the members of informal organizations will simply pursue, often unconsciously, their own objectives irrespective of management's wishes. In such environments, managers may not be aware of the influence and power of these organizations because the employees do not resist doing the jobs for which they were hired. However, they also do not work at improving the performance of their workgroups because doing so would entail disruption of the status quo. Where neither management nor employees are attempting to improve an organization there is little change.

Change, however, is inevitable as the environments in which organizations exist evolve. All changes, including those that may seem trivial, have a cumulative effect on the members of the organization that are perceived as negative by employees. Daily interactions in the workplace necessarily result in friction, hurt feelings, and potentially threatening changes. Employees respond to these interactions individually and as a group through the informal organization. Their negative bias takes its toll on cooperation, creativity, efficiency, productivity, and ultimately profits.

Employee interactions become the basis of processes and attitudes within their informal organizations that eventually reduce the efficiency of the company because, in the absence of skillful management, they are more often than not perceived negatively. In other words, even in situations where employees do not openly resist the directives of management and the owners are content with performance, employees will eventually work less efficiently due to the cumulative effects of their daily interactions. Without intervention through effective communication processes, employee discontent is inevitable.

In the 1920s, Mary Parker Follett addressed the typical reaction employees have to the directives of management. Many employees feel that at least some of their managers' commands are arbitrary. Arbitrary commands ignore an important feature of human nature, which is that people want to govern their own lives. We've heard children say, "Don't boss me around," or "You can't tell me what to do." Although it's rare to hear an adult express this sentiment so directly, every adult was a child once, and none of them have abandoned their desire to govern their own lives. The need for freedom and self-determination is instinctual and powerful.

Nearly every manager will agree that most people don't mind doing what they are told to do, but they intensely dislike being ordered around. This is a key point to understand because more trouble has likely resulted from the manner in which orders are given than any other single factor in the work environment. Employees consider poorly framed directives to be evidence of the harassment, tyrannical conduct, and overbearing nature of management. Instances in which managers are particularly inattentive to the feelings of their subordinates often result in grievances and disrespectful behavior.

It's important to note that even when directives are given sensitively, employees may react against them if they view them as commands. It is the command rather than the action requested that triggers the resentment. An employee will often balk at a directive issued by management when he or she would have immediately and gladly performed the required service if a coworker had requested it. This is the case because it is not the action commanded that is resented but the command itself. Follett noted that in such instances, resistance can be overcome by utilizing the demand of the situation rather than the authority of the manager to direct the employee's conduct. When the situation demands certain action, employees who resent being ordered about will voluntarily undertake the necessary tasks.

The very issuing of orders by managers raises feelings within employees that the orders are arbitrary and that managers are being bossy and controlling just because they can. When employees feel this way, they withhold possible contributions to the workplace, and friction often develops between them and their supervisors. This is a serious drawback because one of the greatest assets a business can have is the employees' pride in their work. If workers disagree with the way they are directed to accomplish tasks, they will often lose interest in the results and make sure that their work will turn out badly. They know their jobs, and they will not be told how to do them.

Follett advocated allowing workers to study the situations in which they and their managers are involved with the idea that the workers' experience is as valuable as the judgments of management in determining what a situation demands. If, for example, a better way to do a particular job is discovered by the research department, workers should be persuaded that the new method really is better and not merely be directed to change methods by their manager.[52] This is preferable according to Follett because it is less likely to interfere with the workers' pride in their work.

While Follett makes quite a bit of good sense in this assessment of workers' distaste for commands, the idea that simply explaining the situation will completely solve problems is naively optimistic. It is correct that discussing the situation with those affected greatly diminishes resentments stemming from the human tendency to resent authority, but it does not take into account the influence of the informal organization. While an explanation may diminish an employee's feelings that a directive is arbitrary, it assumes that the employee has the same objectives as the employer and that he or she wants to cooperate.

This may not be the case for a variety of reasons, one of which is that numerous other directives that employees have been given in the past have been resented. These resentments may have built up among employees to the point that the informal organization is no longer neutral to the objectives of management but now opposes them. Employees will follow Follett's law of the situation only when their behavior is consistent with the objectives and interests of the informal organization to which they belong.

When it is not consistent, they will act in harmony with the attitudes of their coworkers or face negative peer pressure and ostracism. The loss of support of one's coworkers can be devastating for an employee and is, therefore, a very important factor in considering whether to cooperate with management. The way in which a directive is framed is only one factor and, in comparison to the power of the informal organization, a relatively minor one. If managers cannot integrate the interests of their companies and their employees, dissatisfaction will build underground and become a strong factor impeding the success of the entire enterprise. Dissatisfaction will grow behind the scenes and manifest at times and in places where it is least desired and expected. These

---

52   Mary Parker Follett, "Constructive Conflict," *Mary Parker Follett Prophet of Management*, ed. Pauline Graham (Washington D.C.: Beard Books, 2003), 125-126.

surprises are more disruptive and damaging than dealing with the dissatisfaction in the first place.[53]

How exactly does one deal with dissatisfaction building up from the often unpredictable reactions of employees to managers and other employees? Follett was correct in noting the critical need to address dissatisfaction, but offered only general guidance in terms of integrating the interests of management and employees to avoid periodic but serious organizational dysfunction.

Simply being aware of the problem and how it develops is not helpful to managers. While the awareness of the losses to efficiency caused by negative employee attitudes has steadily increased over the years since the time of Follett, progress in the area of how to manage informal organizations has left much to be desired. The main reason managers know so little about how to manage informal employee organizations is that the causes of dissatisfaction in the workplace are notoriously difficult to study scientifically. Elton Mayo was the first to point out the problems inherent in researching this phenomenon.

In the 1930s, Elton Mayo noted the complexity of the variables influencing the performance of employees. He borrowed from the findings of the physiologists of the time that work can be performed only when human beings are in what he termed a steady state. Mayo realized that many mutually dependent variables are responsible for the state of employees.[54] Due to the large number of these variables, employees are in a steady state only rarely and then only temporarily. The cumulative, negative effects of daily interactions on employees are inevitable and virtually ensure that their informal organizations will be neutral toward or unsupportive of company objectives.

Industrial research from the 1930s came to recognize that interferences with the sustained quantity and quality of work in

---

53   Mary Parker Follett, "Coordination," *Mary Parker Follett Prophet of Management*, ed. Pauline Graham (Washington D.C.: Beard Books, 2003), 191.
54   Mayo, *The Human Problems of an Industrial Civilization*, 28.

industry were not primarily organic, but psychological.[55] This discovery turned the attention of researchers to the experimental investigation of individuals at work. They worked to discover and quantify the effects of such factors as monotony, fatigue, and boredom on worker productivity. It was the hope that if the mental state of individual employees could be managed or controlled, the performance of the workgroup could be improved. Employees who consider their work monotonous are typically less productive than those who enjoy it. Fatigued workers do not work as hard as those who have had adequate rest, and monotony itself can generate fatigue.

The industrial studies of the 1920s and 1930s generated surprising results. Researchers found that the conditions prevailing in the various industries of the time were monotonous. This was attributed to the way complex tasks were divided among workers to increase their efficiency. Mayo noted though that although industrial conditions almost certainly did result in monotony for the workers, the amount of monotony they experienced was likely more dependent on their attitude than their working conditions.[56] In other words, the psychological state of monotony was actually more dependent on another psychological state— the worker's attitude toward his or her work rather than the nature of the task itself.

The perception of monotony is subjective. While some workers may find a particular task monotonous to the point of being intolerable, others may find it pleasant. An occupation that may be extremely monotonous to one person may be interesting and rewarding to another. In addition, the same person may find his or her job boring and tedious one day and exciting the next. Internal mental states vary from person to person and within the same individual from time to time.[57] These nebulous and constantly changing mental states form the emotional foundations of

---

55 Ibid., 28.
56 Ibid., 30.
57 Mayo, *The Human Problems of an Industrial Civilization*, 34.

informal organizations in the workplace. In the absence of effective intervention, new employees can acquire negative attitudes from the informal organizations of nearly any company.

The roots of discontent go even deeper. Another factor studied by Mayo and his contemporaries was boredom. They found that the experience of boredom was also dependent on individual psychological characteristics. It was discovered that although workers of superior intelligence were more easily bored, they were nevertheless typically more efficient than their less intelligent coworkers.[58] Although researchers noted that the level of boredom experienced by workers appeared to be related at least somewhat to working conditions, intelligence and attitude have more powerful effects on productivity.

Of course, they found that when activities were varied, the work was perceived as less boring. Also, workers tended to become less bored when they were paid piece rates rather than hourly. Workers' also considered piecework more important because it comprised a series of individual tasks, which was perceived as less boring than work that involved a single interminable activity. Working in groups and taking appropriate breaks also reduced boredom.[59] But the control of these factors could not override the effects of employees' informal organizations.

Although these factors have an effect on boredom in the workplace, their usefulness in improving efficiency is limited as evidenced by the fact that employees with higher intelligence were more efficient despite being more easily bored. These factors are what employees react to within their working environment, but the nature of their reaction is dependent on their attitude toward their work. The psychological state of employees is ultimately of more importance than the events and conditions they react to in the workplace. It all boils down to the attitudes and beliefs of the people doing the work. The psycho-

---

58 Ibid., 32.
59 Ibid., 33.

logical states of employees are influenced more powerfully by their informal organizations than by any other factors within the control of management.

While employees' tolerance for their work varies among individuals of different temperaments and intelligence levels, the personal and social aspects of the groups in which they work influence their efficiency in profound ways.[60] Although Mayo was not aware of informal organizations as such, he discovered their power and effects.

Mayo noted that other researchers had observed similar forces at work in other factories. In one, employee complaints of dullness and monotony abounded, whereas in the other factory, workers appeared to enjoy their work. What was the difference? In the factory in which boredom, poor employee attitudes, and inefficiency prevailed, workers felt that no one took an interest in them, and there was no *esprit de corps*. In the other, the collective attitude of employees was supportive of the objectives of the company because they felt that management took an interest in them and shared their interests.

The work itself and the compensation at both factories were very similar. In the factory with unsupportive employees, the primary motivator was only monetary. In the other, there was real interest in the work and a desire to cooperate with management arising from the social relationships among workers and managers. In the inefficient factory, the informal organization was neutral or mildly negative, whereas in the other, the informal organization was supportive of the objectives of the company.

Workers engaged in repetitive work may be limited in their movements and the scope of their tasks, but their emotional responses are not completely controlled by their work. Their responses are heavily influenced by the informal organization or social network of other employees. When they fail to please one of their peers, they may find support and understanding from

---

60   Mayo, *The Human Problems of an Industrial Civilization*, 35.

another. Employees' social networks provide them with a significant level of independence from the need for approval from their
supervisors, and as such, they heavily influence employees' attitudes toward the tasks they are asked to perform.

When workers experience what they perceive as unwarranted
criticism or injustice at the hands of their superiors, they look to
their fellow workers for support and sympathy. Most employees
are capable of calling on the esprit de corps of their workgroup
to oppose nearly any directive or decision of management. Some
employees find this power satisfying to the point that they search
for some sort of grievance on a regular basis. These situations arise
frequently and change the focus of work from the task and even
from compensation to the emotions aroused among employees
within the workgroup.[61] The social situation involves the entire
informal employee organization.

The roots of discontent among employees are not limited to
monotony, fatigue, and boredom. Both employees and managers
are often at a loss to identify the contributory factors to the pessi-
mism and anger they encounter in the workplace.[62] When neither
management nor employees can articulate just what is responsible for the negative climate dominating their organization, no
amount of planning or research is likely to provide an effective
intervention. Prevailing negative work climates are responsible
for unimaginable losses in efficiency and productivity as well as
unnecessary human suffering.

Collaboration in the workplace is dependent for its success on
the evolution of the emotionally based social code of the informal
organization. This social code or generalized attitude regulates
the interactions of employees within the group toward each other
and with management.[63] The excessive reliance of managers on
economic logic for the control of employee performance is unfortunate. The mere skillful manipulation of monetary incentives is

---

61   Ibid., 37-38.
62   Ibid., 54.
63   Mayo, *The Human Problems of an Industrial Civilization*, 120.

bound to fail if it is incompatible with the social code of the informal organization that has evolved. Attempts to buy loyalty and cooperation only lead to resentment and continued frustration on the part of both employees and management.

In the 1940s, Chester Barnard grappled with the roots of dissatisfaction in the workplace. He noted that all actions of individuals produce both intended and unintended consequences. These consequences produce satisfactions or dissatisfactions for the employees involved even if the purpose of the intended actions is never realized. Highly significant social satisfactions and dissatisfactions arise from cooperative activities themselves regardless of the outcomes. In other words, employees may experience a great deal of satisfaction even though company goals are not attained, and they may experience dissatisfaction even though goals have been met.[64] They do not necessarily respond to company objectives the way managers do even if incentives are designed to secure their cooperation.

Employees may become dissatisfied even though the purposes of their group within the formal organization are achieved; conversely, they may be satisfied even though their group is not performing adequately. This occurs because the informal organization is based on emotions. Employees typically have more socially oriented objectives than task oriented objectives regardless of the incentive structure within their companies. The opposite is true, of course, for managers. Management's main objectives are nearly always task oriented.

Barnard noted that in all organizations, the willingness of members to contribute to the economic objectives of their companies varies widely from individual to individual.[65] This willingness to contribute reflects attitudes that range from an intense desire to further the purposes of the company to absolute hatred of those objectives and complete unwillingness to further them.

---

64 Barnard, *The Functions of the Executive*, 21.
65 Ibid., 84.

He noted that in modern society, the average level of desire to contribute almost always lies on the negative side, and most of the positive contributions in terms of work and creativity come from only a small minority of employees. This is the primary reason that unmanaged informal organizations of employees nearly always have a negative effect on productivity.

Equally important is the fact that the willingness of employees to contribute is not constant but varies over time. It fluctuates necessarily. Of course, it cannot exist during sleep and therefore is diminished by fatigue. It also varies due to the daily flood of perceptions and judgments entailed in the interpersonal interactions required to work within the group. The variance arising from human interactions is largely regulated by the informal organization and the processes at work within it.

Barnard found that most employees are near the neutral point in terms of willingness to contribute to the objectives of their companies or to do their jobs. That is, they are not highly motivated, and at any given moment they may choose to cooperate or refuse to cooperate. Over the course of hours and days, the number of employees with a positive willingness to contribute to company objectives—to perform their jobs well—is constantly fluctuating. This means that the willingness of employees to do their best for their companies will always be unstable.[66] Most companies only rarely even come close to their potential for achieving their objectives because half or more of their employees are not fully willing to do their best.

From the viewpoint of the employee, the willingness to contribute is the cumulative effect of his desires to contribute and to avoid contributing. From the viewpoint of management, the willingness of employees to contribute is a function of economic inducements and burdens imposed. Note the difference here. This is bound to result in frustration for managers because employee performance is ultimately the product of a personal, subjective willingness to

---

66   Ibid., 85-86.

contribute that is not dominated by economic logic. Objective incentives and inducements are effective only if the employees themselves find them satisfying and valuable. What employees find satisfying and valuable is more powerfully influenced by the informal organization of their peers than any objective economic consideration.

The importance of status to employees must also be considered. Status issues often generate discontent in the workplace. In making necessary adjustments in procedures and job assignments, it is relatively easy for managers to inadvertently disturb the equilibrium of status among workers and the pecking order of their informal organization. Actions affecting status tend to disrupt the most powerful and established employees the most, so they are typically the most vocal in opposing change within the company.

Among other things, employees obtain some of their status among their peers from the jobs they perform. Managers will find that nearly any employee will be willing to perform the most menial tasks if status comes with the job. One of the factors evaluated by employees (whether consciously or unconsciously) is the effect that any change in assignment or procedure may have on their status within the group. Although compensation may serve as objective evidence of status for some employees, it is important to remember that status within workgroups is conferred by the informal organization of employees rather than by management, and compensation is determined by management, thus its influence is actually not as powerful. Many managers have been frustrated when an employee is offered more money to change jobs but refuses because he or she views the change in assignment as a demotion notwithstanding the increased compensation.

Managerial actions that may generate status problems are surprisingly varied. Asking employees to work at tasks not covered in their job descriptions may threaten the social structure of the entire informal organization. Seemingly minute changes in working conditions, parking places, office furnishings, reports, and even office location may disturb the established pecking order. Status symbols arising from channels of communication are violated whenever someone fails to follow the expected chain of command or goes over someone's head with a question or complaint. Assigning someone to train new employees or to be consulted in the event of problems or questions has the potential to disturb the established social order.

When employees are faced with conflicting desires regarding whether to cooperate in a change of task that could affect the informal organization, they usually turn to their peers to iron out the question through discussion. They are influenced not only by the objective economic issues of the situation but by the opinions and attitudes of their peers. If employees fear that they will be viewed as "uppity" by their coworkers, they will resist changes in assignment to avoid finding themselves without the support and good will of their coworkers. Since so many variables in the workplace exert significant influences on the social structure of the informal organization, even the most careful managers cannot avoid generating discontent at some point or another.

However, Norman Maier pointed out in the 1950s that it should not be assumed that informal organizations of employees are uniformly undesirable. They are responsible for providing employees with security and facilitating communication within workgroups. Once employees have found their niche within the informal organization of their workgroup, they experience less anxiety and more satisfaction from their interactions with other employees. Employees are insecure and anxious until they have learned the unwritten rules of the informal organization and are accepted by their peers. Since informal organizations are unavoidable components of all businesses, the task is not to attempt to encourage or discourage them, but to learn how to manage and work with them to secure their support within the company.[67]

---

67   Maier, Solem, and Maier, *Supervisory & Executive Development*, 66-67.

In the 1960s, Douglas McGregor revisited the possible roots of discontent in the workplace and noted that when basic needs are met, social needs become more important determinants of human behavior in the workplace. Needs for belonging, being accepted by one's peers, and having friends play dominant roles. While managers are aware of these human needs, they often assume that they are only hindrances to the functioning of the company. This is not the case. Cohesive, emotionally invested employees working together for a common end are much more effective than a group of detached individuals pursing company directives for mere monetary incentives.

The idea that social needs are a source of disruption in the workplace comes from managers' frustration with the informal organizations of employees operating within their companies. When employees' social needs are not met, they are antagonistic toward management and generally uncooperative. They resist change and innovation as they protect their status among their peers. Measures taken by management to weaken this hostility by attempting to interfere with informal group dynamics will only increase the dysfunction. This is because their attempts usually involve manipulating objective incentives such as compensation.

Social needs are only the beginning. McGregor noted that when social needs have been reasonably satisfied in the workplace, egoistic needs assume predominant importance.[68] Egoistic needs relate to self-esteem and status. The needs for self-esteem include the desire for self-respect, confidence, freedom within the workplace, high levels of skill, and continuous learning. The needs for recognition and the respect of others also relate to status. McGregor postulated that these needs are never satisfied and that human beings will go on seeking satisfaction indefinitely once enough lower level needs have been satisfied to allow them

---

68   Douglas McGregor, *The Human Side of Enterprise*, annotated ed., Joel Cutcher-Gershenfeld, ed. (New York: McGraw-Hill, 2006), 49-51.

to become important. This means that egoistic needs are here to stay, and they can be powerful motivators when they are managed systematically.

These needs play an important role in the development of chronic discontent in the workplace because industrial organizations offer very limited opportunities for their satisfaction. In fact, the typical responses of management to systemic resistance and antagonism actually interfere with the satisfaction of self-actualizing employee needs. This unfortunate result only increases discontent within companies and drives dysfunction underground where it festers and gains strength. For companies to reach their full potential in terms of their ability to accomplish their missions, their employees must be able to satisfy their needs for self-fulfillment. The ability of every employee to realize his or her potential for self-development is linked intimately to the success of the company. This shared interest is what makes managing employee attitudes and their informal organizations possible.

Many managers make the error of relying exclusively on motivation through carefully planned economic incentives. Interestingly, the monetary rewards offered are useful for satisfying employees' needs only away from the workplace. Other than indirectly through the status money can confer, monetary rewards do little to satisfy self-actualizing needs. Consider wages, for example. Strictly speaking, wages can be spent only after work. They have very limited social value in the work setting and are notoriously inefficient motivators. A person will work hard to impress a coworker if the coworker supports the mission of the company. However, if coworkers scorn the mission of the company and management, the same person will withhold enough effort to fit in. It is social suicide to become known as a "brown-noser."

A higher rate of pay is largely irrelevant to employees unless it contributes to the status of the job and the employee holding that job. If higher compensation is effective at all, it is because of its contribution to the satisfaction of the employee's self-actualizing needs. Unfortunately, when rates of pay are powerful, they typically generate unexpected consequences for management. McGregor cited this as the reason that small and objectively insignificant differences in the rates of compensation can result in heated debate and distraction in the workplace.[69] The issue is not economic, but psychological. It's not what the higher wages can buy that determines their power, but the status those wages confer on the ones earning them. Any misunderstanding of this is likely to result in controversy and dissatisfaction. The same is true of most fringe benefits offered to employees such as overtime, vacation, medical benefits, and profit sharing plans. Employee dissatisfaction cannot be effectively managed with economic incentives alone.

Since most economic rewards are deferred and available only when the employee is away from the job, it should not be surprising that they are not as powerful as the social rewards employees obtain while they are working together. While management's attempts to manipulate incentives to control employee behavior often become sources of discontent, they do not have as much influence on employee attitudes and performance as peer pressure, acceptance, and status, all of which are factors largely controlled and dispensed by the informal organizations of employees.

Informal organizations offer opportunities for employees to satisfy their self-actualizing social and egoistic needs. When these needs are not met, employees are not content, and they express their dissatisfaction through their work. Rarely does management capitalize on the power of informal organizations to motivate employees. When resistance progresses to levels that become apparent to management, the typical response is to resort to economic rewards and punishments or threats. The carrot-and-stick approach has been proven repeatedly to be ineffective in motivating employees. While employees may respond as expected initially, they will ultimately look for other jobs or find ways to get even through sabotage and soldiering.

---

69   Ibid., 53-54.

Management techniques relying solely on direction and control do not motivate employees to make their best contribution to the objectives of the business. These approaches are ineffective because they rely on satisfying only the lower level needs of employees. When employees have attained reasonable levels of job security and compensation, they attaint a level of independence from most of the economically based incentives and disincentives wielded by management. Employees increasingly look to work for the satisfaction of their self-actualizing social and egoistic needs, and these needs are satisfied by their informal organization rather than by management.

When there are few opportunities to satisfy these self-actualizing needs at work, employees become lazy, passive, antagonistic, and unwilling to follow the directives of management.[70] Their responses to incentive programs may seem irrational to managers when they appear to ignore objective, economic incentives. A typical example of this phenomenon occurs when a well-designed economic incentive is received enthusiastically by one department, but is spurned by another department within the same company. This can occur because the level of support of the informal organizations within the two departments differs. In one department, the informal organization is supportive while in the other it is discontented and hostile.

In summary, then, how exactly do the roots of discontent, which plague employees and managers alike, become established? The answer is that they develop naturally through the day-to-day interactions of employees and managers. Discontent is the byproduct of both the intentional and unintentional actions of people working together. Every thoughtless, irritating, and inconsiderate interaction makes its contribution.[71] The everyday push and shove, the uncaring remark taken personally, and the desire to be autonomous and respected inevitably lead to discontent in the

---

70   McGregor, *The Human Side of Enterprise*, 54-55.
71   Philip B. Crosby, *Quality without Tears: The Art of Hassle-Free Management* (New York: McGraw-Hill, 1984), 15.

absence of a well-managed informal organization. In other words, dysfunctional informal employee organizations are the norm in the absence of effective managerial interventions. Motivational strategies based on the lower level economic needs of employees are of little help in addressing the negative attitudes that grow within informal organizations.

4.

THE POWER OF THE INFORMAL ORGANIZATION

The culture of an organization results from the interaction of the formal and informal organizations that comprise it. For example, a decision by management to increase employee participation in planning and decision-making processes may foster a cooperative informal organization that is supportive of the objectives of the company. However, attempts by management staff to break the informal organization by firing ringleaders suspected of being responsible for the poor attitudes of other employees often result in defensive, uncooperative informal organizations that resist and sabotage the mission of the company.

The organizational culture can also nurture or harm the employees subject to it. High rates of divorce and absenteeism among employees often signal problems within the informal organization. For example, high rates of divorce among employees may result from an organizational culture that is unnecessarily competitive due to the formal design of its reward structure. Management's awareness of the power of informal organizations is the first prerequisite to the development of a supportive and cooperative culture within any company.

Informal organizations have a profound influence on the frequency and nature of conflicts within companies. Infrequent, minor conflicts merely reduce efficiency while frequent, significant conflicts can nearly paralyze companies. Conflict is inevitable and occurs both among employees and between employees and managers. Those involved respond in different ways and, in some companies, develop dysfunctional coping mechanisms that generate more serious conflicts in the future. Conflict is a natural byproduct when people work together, and it cannot be ignored.

Consider a situation in which a manager loses patience with an employee and reprimands him or her. Angered, the employee not only does not work as efficiently as before but even wastes time spreading rumors in an attempt to gain the support of coworkers against the manager. The resulting emotion, misinformation, and anger tend to spread to other employees and generate additional conflicts and grievances. Misinformation confuses the focus of employees and affects the interpretation of subsequent events. Employees interpret events and give meaning to their interactions in accordance with their perceptions of reality. These perceptions are in large measure formed by their interactions with their peers within the informal employee network. Since managers are effectively excluded from this network, employees are free to voice their versions of events to their peers regardless of the accuracy of their stories.

In the 1920s, Mary Parker Follett addressed the issue of conflict in the workplace and noted that conflict by itself is neither good nor bad. Enlightened managers often think of it not as warfare, but as the manifestation of differences in opinion or views. Differences of opinion indicate the emotional involvement and interest of employees. Disagreements cannot be avoided in any situation where people need to cooperate and work together.[72] Even if disagreements could be eliminated, the resulting apathy would be even deadlier to efficiency because there is no energy to improve the situation when apathy prevails. If managers can harness the energy of constructive disagreement, they can use it to increase efficiency and productivity as well as build a supportive corporate culture.

Because differences are inevitable, managers should use them proactively instead of fearing them. Unfortunately, many

---

72   Mary Parker Follett, "Constructive Conflict," *Mary Parker Follett Prophet of Management*, ed. Pauline Graham (Washington D.C.: Beard Books, 2003), 67-68.

managers attempt to deal with conflict by domination or compromise. Neither of these approaches is successful. At best, they only produce temporary relief. When differences spread to the point of involving significant numbers of employees in the workplace, the informal organization itself becomes involved in sensitizing employees and influencing their responses to management. Managers really cannot dominate their employees since the employees function within the existence of their informal social networks, and efforts on the part of management to attain compromise based on economic logic will eventually fail. Informal organizations of employees are too powerful for managers to overcome.

Unfortunately, domination often appears to be the quickest and easiest way to deal with conflicts. Managers seduced by this tactic rely on their authority to decide issues in controversy. Unfortunately, this only interferes with employees' expression of their conflicts by driving them underground. The conflicts don't go away. One side has an apparent victory over the other, but the losing party will continue to bear resentment while being in a position to recruit support for his position behind the scenes. As he gathers allies, he can express his resentment through his work by soldiering and sabotaging the efforts of his manager and other employees. While managers are not in a position to check this behavior, the informal organization of employees could be if it were adequately supportive of the company.

Dealing with conflict through compromise is similarly ineffective although it seems to dispense with winners and losers. The theory behind compromise is that if each side gives up a little, the work can continue without being interrupted by the conflict. This is deceptive because neither side is satisfied. Once again, conflicts are driven underground while the parties or factions watch for other opportunities to seek dominance. Despite the popularity of compromise among managers dealing with conflicts, it only postpones the fight. Ultimately, the underlying issues must be addressed to the mutual satisfaction of all parties.

Where compromise has been formally adopted as the accepted method for conflict resolution, complex written and unwritten rules have evolved governing how the parties should behave during negotiations. For example, in collective bargaining it is understood that the union will ask for more than it expects and management will offer less than they would otherwise give willingly. The union hopes to arrive at a settlement it can live with after having its demands reduced while management expects a settlement for more than they offered. However, neither side really knows what the other side wants, and neither union nor management can tell the other without disrupting the accepted rules of the game. This ignorance is a great barrier to dealing with conflict in any constructive way.

While compromise is an accepted way of dealing with conflict, it only produces additional friction between management and employees. No one really wants a compromise because it requires giving up something. What really happens is that managers wind up with two losers that simply agree to end the controversy for the time being while they work to increase their bargaining positions. Both parties bear resentments, and the same issues will resurface when one of the parties feels that its position has improved. The cycle repeats itself. The amount of energy and creativity wasted by the parties on garnering support and improving their bargaining positions is staggering. The focus becomes the relative power of the parties rather than the mission of their departments and companies.

Mary Follett advocated accepting conflict as a natural expression of interest in what's going on in the workplace and integrating the interests and desires of managers and employees instead of resorting to domination or compromise.[73] When the desires of both parties are integrated, no one has to sacrifice anything. There is no compromise and no need to increase relative power within the company. The solutions produced recognize the legitimate

---

73   Ibid., 68-69.

interests of both parties and free them to use their full creativity and effort in furthering their shared objectives. These objectives are ultimately the objectives of the company because if the company isn't successful, there will be no divisions within it to disagree.

When managers use the strategy of compromise, the informal organization brings the conflict up again because its members did not really consent to give up a part of their desires. Frustration over giving up something builds underground until it resurfaces in another conflict. The new conflict may involve the same issues that were compromised, or it may arise out of seemingly unrelated issues because the original issues were addressed in the absence of the underlying reasons for the conflict. Compromise fails to engage the informal organization of employees as a whole. The power of the informal organization is not directed toward company objectives through the processes of compromise.

Integration of the objectives of employees' informal organizations with their companies will stabilize the social processes in the workplace. This does not entail the end of change or conflict, however. What is does mean is that the next time a conflict occurs, it will be addressed at a higher level with less anger and less disruption of work.[74] When conflicts do arise, they will involve new issues, and the periods between conflicts will not be used to increase the relative bargaining positions of the parties. Each time a conflict arises, its underlying causes will be addressed to the satisfaction of both parties. The frequency of conflicts and severity will decrease dramatically.

When the conflicts amount to nothing more than differences of opinion, the informal organization will support efforts to address the real issues involved. This significant social progress allows the informal organization to support the mission of the company without reservation. Conflict becomes an opportunity to improve efficiency and productivity while reaffirming the shared objectives

---

74   Ibid., 72-73.

of both management and employees. It leads to invention and the creation of jointly held values and beliefs, and both employees and managers typically welcome it as a sign that conditions will improve for all concerned.

Having identified the integration of desires as a superior way to deal with conflict, the question of how to do this naturally arises. Follett correctly identified improved communication as the key. She advocated management's putting all its cards on the table to bring the entire conflict into the open. When all of the facts are known by both parties, the real issues behind the conflict can be examined. Full disclosure creates an opportunity for both sides to reevaluate their position and values, and it encourages trust. Employees do not feel manipulated when management shares vital information with them, and this feeling of security frees them to utilize the energy they typically would have directed toward protecting their interests to solving the problems they share with management.

It is human nature to assume the validity and rationality of our desires until another desire or need conflicts with it. For example, our desires change as we age. Our immature desires are abandoned as we get older and realize that those desires are not compatible with our changing social and material needs. We desire something but do not estimate how much we really want it until it comes in conflict with another desire. When this occurs and we compare our two desires, we revalue the objects of our desire in light of our current circumstances.

This is what really happens when effective communication processes allow management and employees to integrate their desires in a conflict. Neither side really gives in. What actually happens is that both sides have an opportunity to reevaluate their positions and revalue their desires. The outcome is the unification of the objectives, desires, and interests of both the company and the informal organizations within it. This explains why companies with supportive employee networks are so much more efficient than those impeded by negative ones.

Unfortunately, Follett's suggestions were not detailed enough to provide a clear idea of just what communication processes are effective or how to design them. Her comments were primarily directed to the need for them. Managers were left with an understanding of the problem of integration of interests, but without instructions for addressing it. Further, she took the position that integration was not possible in every situation. Because she did not have a clear idea of how to structure effective communication processes, she concluded that the competing interests in some conflicts could not be integrated. Despite her revolutionary insights into the psychology of the workplace, she was mistaken regarding how effective communication can be in addressing internal company conflicts.

In actuality, integration of interests is possible in virtually every situation in which the informal organization of employees has not been alienated to the point that it is bent on the destruction of the company within which it has evolved. As long as the company is viable, it is possible to integrate the conflicting interests of employees and managers. Effective communication processes engage informal organizations in problem solving when conflicts arise and produce cooperation, understanding, and opportunities for creative improvement. Companies threatened by potentially disruptive change or conflict thrive when they have the support of their employees to deal with the crisis. When managers choose not to engage their employees' social networks in their mission or simply do not know how, all concerned pay a heavy psychological and economic price.

Follett was correct in advocating the use of the energy that conflict generates to further the objectives of the company. One of her key concepts was that management should never ask which party to a conflict is "right." Instead, the proper position for management to take is to assume that all views are correct in some way. This allows all voices to be legitimately heard and considered. When all of the cards are on the table, nothing is driven underground to reduce cooperation or generate morale-killing rumors. Questions are answered and the lack of information is admitted.

When management adopts this posture, the group's effort is directed toward discovering the nature of what is real. The underlying principle is that those who oppose an idea are taking a rational, defensible position. This orientation frees those involved to discover the real issue, integrate their interests, and deal with the situation in a new and creative way. A solution to problems can be found that both sides view as correct without one side losing something to the other.[75]

These ideas were elaborated by Chester Barnard in the 1940s. He took the position that company concerns do not incite cooperative activity unless they are adopted by the employees. Unless objectives are simultaneously accepted by both the formal and informal organizations of a company, there is little willingness to cooperate.[76] Unfortunately, many managers are not aware of this. They believe that employees will embrace company directives, goals, and missions simply because it's the company who issues their paycheck. They blame resistance on the part of groups of employees as petty, irrational, and mean-spirited.

Actions taken by managers usually entail two types of decisions.[77] Decisions of the first type are made within the formal organization of management. These decisions are impersonal and made from a global viewpoint based on the interests of the company as a whole. They are related to the objectives for which the company was created in the first place. They are rationally and economically based and impersonal in both intent and expected effects.

Decisions of the second type are made within the informal organization of the company by each employee affected by

---

75   Follett, "Constructive Conflict," *Mary Parker Follett Prophet of Management*, 75.
76   Barnard, *The Functions of the Executive*, 86.
77   Ibid., 187-188.

management's action. Each employee decides whether to give or withhold cooperation. Whether an employee will contribute to the objectives of the company is a matter of each employee's personal choice. The sum of these individual decisions becomes the informal organization's stance toward goals of the company and the directives of management. The stance of the informal organization then becomes a powerful factor in the level of cooperation of employees on the issues in question and future issues as well. The level of commitment that employees have to their companies is powerfully influenced by the collective opinions of their peers.

Barnard found that the power of incentives rests in the employees' needs for self-preservation and self-satisfaction. Business organizations can function only when their objectives are consistent with the satisfaction of these powerful needs.[78] Employees must be induced to cooperate or their companies will perish. However, the incentives related to self-preservation are not as effective as those based on the self-actualizing egoistic needs of employees. The economic incentives relied on almost exclusively by management are not nearly as effective as those mediated by the employees' informal organizations. Inadequate and poorly managed incentives lead to dysfunction and ultimately dissolution due to lack of cooperative effort.

While managers can award or withhold objective, economic incentives, they have little control over the egoistic incentives mediated by the employees' social networks. Most of the time, the determination of satisfactions and dissatisfactions is not a matter of logical thought or rational economic choices.[79] They are matters of the employees' perceptions based on their own feelings and the perceived feelings, opinions, and attitudes of their peers. Satisfaction is largely determined by the informal organization. This is the reason that an incentive that is effective in one

---

78 Ibid., 139.
79 Barnard, *The Functions of the Executive*, 140.

department of a company can be totally ineffective in another department of the same company. The difference lies not in the incentive but in the attitudes and values of the informal organizations operating in the two departments.

The differences between objective and subjective aspects of various incentives are striking.[80] Material incentives such as money, goods, and services have objective existence as do factors such as working hours and working conditions. From a strictly logical point of view, these incentives should be powerful because they are real. However, the value or power of these motivators is determined subjectively by the employees. If employees feel that the amount of money offered is inadequate, they may actually be insulted by an attempt to reward increased productivity. If they feel their work is important, they may dismiss poor working conditions as unimportant or actually welcome them as a badge of dedication to "the cause."

Because the incentives controlled by management are economic, they are aimed at the lower order needs of employees related to self-preservation and security.[81] However, their power is minimal because the lower order needs of employees have typically been met at least to the point of offering them some level of independence. Objectively valuable incentives can be used to motivate employees to a point, but they are less effective when employees have had their lower order needs met. In most companies, the needs for self-preservation and security are met as a matter of course. Physical safety and predictable compensation come with nearly every job.

The power of informal employee organizations comes from their mediation of the self-actualizing incentives concerned with meeting egoistic needs. Being accepted and respected by one's peers, being part of the "in crowd," and being able to influence the conduct of coworkers are powerful motivators. The opinions of peers regulate both these self-actualizing incentives and they

---

80   Ibid., 141-142.
81   Ibid., 142-143.

determine how employees view the subjective value of many other incentives. Rather than risk social isolation and loss of status within the group, employees will reject offers of economic incentives if their peers don't approve of those incentives.

If the informal organization within a given work environment does not sufficiently value the material incentives controlled by management, they will be ineffective to motivate employees. An example of this occurs when management attempts to increase productivity by offering piece rates to increase output. If the informal organization accepts this, employees will respond with increased production. If it does not, employees will scorn the incentive and punish any employee who attempts to participate in the program. Since different informal organizations exist in virtually every department and plant, the same incentive program may succeed in one location and fail miserably in another.

Informal organizations actually influence the states of mind of their members. They are active in how employees react to the incentive programs designed by management. Incentives must be both objectively and subjectively valuable to employees to be effective. Successful managers need a way to insure that their motivators are valuable in both dimensions. It is common to design incentive programs that are powerful in only one dimension or the other. For example, most industrial organizations rely almost exclusively on the objective value of material incentives, while charitable organizations tend to rely more on the subjective value of social incentives. For maximum effectiveness, incentive programs need to offer employees benefits in both areas.

Barnard referred to the reliance on incentives with objective value as "the method of incentives" and the reliance on social incentives with subjective value as "the method of persuasion." By using the method of persuasion, objective incentives may be rendered effective or ineffective, both methods must be used within successful organizations. Either method by itself will lose effectiveness over time. This is evidenced by the high rate of turnover among employees in low status jobs where objective incentives are the primary motivators, and among volunteers in charitable organizations where social incentives are dominant.

In contrast, the employees of many of the most effective and powerful organizations cooperate with management in environments in which material incentives are either lacking or absent altogether. For example, military organizations are relatively lacking in material incentives. In combat, even basic needs for safety, security, and comfort may be lacking. Nevertheless, the people involved actually work harder for the organization, take more risks, and sacrifice more than they would for any material incentive. Political and religious organizations function similarly.

Material rewards are effective only to a limited extent. Most people can be induced by them only to devote a mere fraction of their possible contribution if they are the only incentives offered by the organization. Material incentives are weak and only minimally effective in the absence of social incentives provided by informal organizations.[82] Social incentives that meet the self-actualizing needs of employees are distributed through the employees' social network that operates within the workplace.

These motivators are essential in the procurement of employee cooperation above a minimal level, and this is the foundation of the power and importance of informal organizations. Opportunities to achieve distinction, prestige, and domination are much more motivating than most of the material incentives offered to the employees by management, and as we discussed earlier, material incentives can only be enjoyed after the employee has left the work setting. For this reason, material motivators are dependent on their power, at least in part, on the status given to them within the informal organization of employees.

For example, relatively small material rewards have the power to produce increased performance and cooperation or jealousy

---

82   Barnard, *The Functions of the Executive*, 144.

and internal strife when they are associated with higher social status.[83] In fact, higher social status is generally presumed to follow the attainment of even minimally greater material rewards. Increasing an employee's compensation above that of his or her peers generally signals increased prestige and higher status within the group. However, if the informal organization does not support the distinction, an increase in pay can result in ostracism and resentment.

The real value of small differences in compensation among employees lies in the recognition and increased status conferred by their peers. Even seemingly insignificant raises given to one employee or one class of employees over another will produce powerful effects when the informal organization supports management's compensation program. Similarly, offers of significant increases in compensation will lack motivational value or will even be perceived as provocations when the employee social network is unsupportive of such an action. Employees' informal organizations actually have the power to make or break any incentive or compensation plan formulated by management.

Chester Barnard went far in explaining this in his discussion of the most powerful motivators at work in companies. Among the most powerful motivators for cooperation are what he termed "ideal benefactions." To the extent that companies can satisfy the personal non-material, emotional desires of employees, they have the ability to provide ideal benefactions. Examples of positive ideal benefactions include satisfying employees' needs for pride in their work, needs for confidence in their ability to solve problems, and needs to altruistically serve a greater cause such as family, religious, or patriotic groups. On the negative side, ideal benefactions may also include the satisfaction of needs to act on hate or take revenge. As is the case for most motivators that satisfy self-actualizing needs, ideal benefactions are largely controlled by employees' peer groups and social networks.

---

83   Ibid., 145-146.

Another powerful motivator recognized by Barnard as critically important was what he termed "associational attractiveness." Associational attractiveness is related to social compatibility.[84] Hostility based on race, social class, and national origin can decrease efficiency or even destroy cooperation within any formal organization. In some instances, businesses must resort to increasing material incentives to counteract the dysfunctional effects of negative associational attractiveness.

Unfortunately, these have limited effectiveness because associational attractiveness and ideal benefactions are defined and mediated by informal organizations, not by management. Since they are largely controlled by the informal organizations of employees, the introduction of ever more complex and costly material reward programs to deal with the dysfunction they cause are doomed from the outset. Managers cannot ignore the power of informal employee organizations. The objective incentives controlled by management address only the lower level needs of employees and are desirable from an economic point of view. The social motivators controlled by the employees' informal organization address self-actualizing needs and are emotionally desirable. Most people will not work well and some will not work at all despite material incentives for cooperation if the social situation from their point of view is not satisfactory.[85]

Of course, the assumption behind the use of economic incentives is that employees will work harder for more money. This rationale is based on an economic logic that presumes that employees will behave rationally. Accordingly, managers establish productivity standards for their employees and determine scales of incentive pay to provide bonuses for employees exceeding their standards. The problem with this assumption is that it fails to take into account other more powerful social forces operating within their organizations.

---

84   Ibid., 145-146.
85   Barnard, *The Functions of the Executive*, 147.

These forces include the peer pressure and public opinion exerted by employees' social networks. Most employees want the approval of their coworkers and will even give up bonuses or, in extreme cases, accept reduced compensation to attain it. The introduction of piece rates is usually rejected by employees when their coworkers as a group believe that piece rates or other incentives will be reduced once productivity has been increased. When the informal organization of employees does not support piece rate programs, the employees will actually believe that they will be working harder for the same pay. When the informal organization opposes company programs, even average workers are clever enough to defeat any system of controls devised by management.

Successful incentive plans may bring about moderate increases in productivity, but they also give birth to dysfunctional employee behaviors aimed at protecting their interests. These include soldiering, sabotage, inaccurate record keeping and reporting, and excessive filing of grievances with management. If employee suspicions and concerns are not addressed by managers, incentive plans that appear to be successful initially will typically result in widespread antagonism and diminished cooperation.

The outcomes of incentive programs that are not supported by employees are costly to companies that rely exclusively on material incentives to secure the cooperation of their employees. What is more, managements' responses to these outcomes usually exacerbate the problems they cause. In the 1960s, Douglas McGregor determined that if the direct and indirect costs of administering most incentive programs could be tallied, they would more than outweigh any resulting gains from productivity.[86] Due to the generalized lack of support from informal organizations operating within companies, most incentive programs cannot work well, do not work at all, or actually interfere with management-employee cooperation.

The informal organizations at work within every business do not acquire their power from the ability to provide material incentives

---

86   McGregor, *The Human Side of Enterprise*, 11-12.

to their members. They have no direct control over wages, hours, or working conditions. Their power lies in their ability to change the desires of their members and mediate employee perceptions. They actually control to some extent how employees value the incentives offered by management. This is why the same compensation program can be viewed as satisfactory by most employees in one plant or department and totally unacceptable in another.

This persuasive power of informal organizations comes from their ability to create and maintain coercive conditions for their members.[87] This is accomplished through peer pressure applied directly or indirectly. Peer pressure to accept the values, beliefs, and social structure of a group can take the form of open hostility or ostracism. Forced exclusion of any employee from the social workgroup generates fear even in those not directly involved. Employees are faced with the alternatives of going along with the group or losing the benefits of positive association with their coworkers.

Informal organizations also influence the cooperation of their members in the pursuit of formal company objectives through their impact on the acceptability of the orders issued by management. It is generally recognized that when management must give orders to employees that are likely to be unacceptable to them, additional work will be necessary on the part of management.[88] This additional effort generally takes the form of education, logical persuasion, or the offering of incentives. This is necessary to avoid the employees' disobedience and denial of management's authority.

New, relatively inexperienced managers are often guilty of assuming their instructions will be followed in the absence of this groundwork. When they fail to take adequate steps prior to issuing controversial directives, the workgroup is partially disorganized due to the resulting dysfunction and conflict. Experienced executives who are seduced by the delusion of power also tend to disorganize their workgroups in much the same way. Disorganization

---

87   Barnard, *The Functions of the Executive*, 149.
88   Ibid., 168.

reduces productivity, task focus and cooperation that continues until the group readjusts. In some companies, employee groups are nearly constantly in the readjustment process because of inept management and a failure to effectively work with the informal organization among the employees.

This well-known phenomenon relates directly to the acceptability of orders and directives. The acceptability of managerial orders lies along a continuum ranging from those that certainly will not be obeyed to those than are unquestionably acceptable. Between these two extremes is a neutral area where orders are either barely acceptable or barely unacceptable. Barnard called the area of acceptability where orders will almost certainly be obeyed the "zone of indifference."[89] Employees receiving orders within this zone are relatively indifferent to those orders as long as the person making them has the requisite authority. This is in contrast to orders outside the neutral zone, which are questioned, scrutinized, and discussed, and usually only grudgingly obeyed.

What is interesting here is that the zone of indifference expands and contracts depending on the level of support within the informal organizations of a company. The types of orders that will be accepted will be very limited among employees, and will only barely induce them to cooperate when their social network does not embrace the mission of the company. Employees who are members of a supportive group and are highly devoted to a company have a much broader zone of indifference. Since the efficiency of companies is directly affected by the degree to which employees assent to orders, the size of the zone of indifference is critical, and informal organizations command the power to define it.

The size of the zone of indifference varies with each employee and even varies within the same employee over a time, but it is heavily influenced by the informal organization to which the employee belongs. These socially based organizations affect the attitude and values of each of their members. People are influenced by public

89   Ibid., 168-170.

opinion and the feelings of their coworkers in profound ways. When the informal organization as a whole finds a given directive within the zone of indifference, very few members of the work-group will question it. To do so invites the disapproval of fellow workers and a great deal of negative attention.

It is really a sort of fiction to believe that authority comes down from above in an organization. This idea is based on the false assumption that orders from superiors will be acceptable and employees will obey them without feeling as though they are sacrificing their personal freedom or losing their status within the informal organization. It presumes that employees always take orders without taking them personally.

The extent of the zone of indifference is largely set by the informal organization operating within a group. When it is restricted due to the ill-advised actions of managers, cooperation is encumbered and efficiency is lost. When it is expanded, companies experience unprecedented cooperation and efficiency as employees work with managers and vice versa to achieve the objectives of both the company and the informal organizations within it.

In the 1950s, Norman Maier noted that the decisions of management are better accepted by employees when they have had a voice in their formulation. When employees are involved in decision-making, their informal organization is engaged in pursuing the objectives of the company even as it pursues its own. This is another manifestation of the power of informal organizations at work. Their influence on their members is profound. A long recognized way to engage the informal organization is to obtain employee participation in problem solving. When this strategy is employed, supervisors openly discuss problems with their employees. When issues are skillfully presented, employees can provide an important resource for solving recurring problems that plague management.[90]

---

90   Maier, Solem, and Maier, *Supervisory & Executive Development*, 111-112.

Engaged employees are aware of the current reality of their working environments. They consider potential solutions to problems in light of organizational strengths, weaknesses, and obstacles. They capitalize on the positive qualities of the organization to solve problems. Group weaknesses that can be improved are addressed by the employees themselves. Supportive employees consider situations that cannot be improved as challenges to be circumvented in dealing with company problems. Supportive informal employee organizations give employees the freedom to address their companies' challenges with creative problem solving.

Employee participation in problem solving engages the informal organizations by sharing the ownership of the problems addressed. This is an effective strategy because it allows members of the informal organization to reconsider their views of organizational realities. It provides opportunities for employees to meet some of their self-actualizing social needs in the workplace by supporting the mission of the company. If this is done on a sufficiently broad scale, the informal organizations themselves become supportive of management. When informal organizations own the company's problems and the proposed measures undertaken to solve them, they own the success or failure of those measures as well.

Informal organizations exert a powerful influence on the productivity of their formal organizations. This is evidenced by the fact that, generally speaking, highly cohesive groups are more productive than less cohesive groups.[91] In cohesive workgroups, employees and their managers trust and like one another. This is only possible in workgroups in which the informal organization of employees allows it. The power of informal employee social networks to influence productivity in the workplace comes from their ability to influence the perceptions of employees relating appropriate levels of support, trust, and role expectations. With the

---

91   B. Mullen and C. Copper, "The relation between group cohesiveness and performance: An integration," *Psychological Bulletin*, 115, no. 2 (1994): 210-227.

ability to influence employee perceptions of the value of incentives, status, cooperation, and trust, informal organizations have unrivaled power to enhance or discourage cohesiveness in the companies in which they have evolved.

The importance of cohesiveness is difficult to exaggerate because it has an important influence on the degree to which organizational goals are accepted by its members as well as on productivity.[92] Along with the power to enhance employee performance within companies, informal employee organizations also have the power to sabotage it notwithstanding management's control of wages, hours, and working conditions. Non-supportive informal organizations will pursue the emotional interests of their members even though they are perceived as inconsistent with the objectives of the company and irrational from an economic standpoint.

The power of informal organizations is considerable and presents both a threat and an opportunity for managers. When ignored, these informal employee organizations tend to diminish the efficiency of the formal organizations in which they have evolved. When properly managed, they have the power to enlist the creativity and energy of employees in the pursuit of company goals to an extent most companies have never experienced. The issue at stake is how managers of rationally based formal organizations can influence the supportiveness and cohesiveness of emotionally based and loosely organized informal employee organizations. The key to the management of informal employee organizations lies in communication processes that free employees to focus their creativity and energy on issues that promote the economic interests of their companies as they pursue satisfaction of their self-actualizing needs.

92　P. M. Podsakoff, , S. B. MacKenzie, and M. Ahearne, "Moderating effects of goal acceptance on the relationship between group cohesiveness and productivity," *Journal of Applied Psychology*, 82, no. 6 (1997): 974-983.

5.

LISTENING TO THE REAL ISSUES

While the power of informal organizations has been recognized at least from as early as the turn of the twentieth century, specific methods for managing informal organizations have not been developed systematically. One reason for this is that informal organizations are not planned entities that respond to economic logic. They are the groups of employees responsible for the collective emotional reactions, values, and customs that arise among employees through their interactions with management and each other. The power structure within them is not clearly delineated on organizational charts, and it is difficult for managers to anticipate the emotional and status-based relationships that thrive among employees.

While the collective opinions expressed when employees apply peer pressure to each other are known to exist, it is often difficult for managers to learn what they are. Most of the techniques available to managers rely on material incentives to motivate employees. Admittedly, these techniques are somewhat effective and are responsible for the limited success observed in most industries today. Unfortunately, however, they do not engage informal organizations and fall far short of capitalizing on their power to marshal employee devotion, good will, and creativity.

Beginning with this chapter, we will discuss a group of techniques and strategies capable of engaging informal organizations successfully. They can be used individually or in combination as the need arises. However, it is recommended that they be used together to garner the support of the informal organization of employees. As employees and managers become accustomed to these communication processes, formal adherence to the recommended order of processes can be relaxed and individual techniques can be used in isolation to deal with specific problems. The communication processes capable of managing informal organizations include group listening, goal setting, vision development, integration of objectives, and continuous communication. In combination, these techniques serve as an effective group problem-solving technique that can be used continuously.

When these processes are combined and used as a single intervention, they result in a plan for the informal organization of employees. This is a blueprint for the integration of the objectives of the company and the informal employee organizations within it. For this reason, we will refer to these plans as organizational integration plans throughout the remainder of this book. These plans should not be confused with strategic plans.

Strategic plans are products of the combined logic, experience, and expertise of managers. In short, they are indispensible parts of the formal system. However, they state and further the objectives of management and have little to do with the emotionally based objectives of the employees comprising the informal organization. Most of the difficulties in implementing strategic plans arise because their objectives and procedures are viewed as inconsistent with the interests of the employees charged with implementing them, i.e. the informal organization.

While strategic plans change the functioning of the formal organization, organizational integration plans manage the attitudes and values of employees. Where management provides planning and material incentives to encourage the cooperation of employees, the informal organization provides social incentives that are often more powerful than the economic incentives that can be offered by management. In addition, the informal organization has the power to actually change the perceived value of both material and social incentives—the power to determine what will and what will not function as incentives as well as how effective any given incentives will be.

Strategic planning is a powerful technique aimed at determining the changes that should be made in the formal system. Organizational integration can be accomplished through a cluster of techniques that facilitates the implementation of the strategic plan. Organizational integration is used to manage the informal organization's response to the directives of management. The ongoing implementation processes of integration allow workgroups to adjust to changing conditions through healthy communication and integrate both the formal and informal objectives of the group.

The communication processes that build organizational integration can also be used to solve problems in large groups ranging from a single department to an entire division or plant. The individual techniques that comprise this integration process can be utilized at every level of management to address specific symptoms of organizational dysfunction. These techniques provide management with a means of integrating the objectives of both the formal and informal organizations of employees and harnessing previously untapped creativity, energy and support for the mission of the company.

The symptoms of dysfunction originating with the informal organization include generalized low morale, petty squabbling, resistance to management directives and lack of respect for managers, doing the least amount of work possible, and soldiering or only pretending to work. Even in the absence of these symptoms, communication strategies aimed at the integration of organizational objectives typically increase efficiency. The consistent failure of workgroups to meet their goals signals that one or more of the techniques of organizational integration will be effective either in the revision of the goals or in freeing employees to reach them.

Organizational integration techniques are especially useful in times of significant change such as mergers, reorganizations, consolidations, liquidations, downsizing, and modernization. These techniques can be used to advantage by new managers to develop the legitimacy of their leadership and secure the active support of the informal organizations operating within their companies. The integration of organizational objectives reduces stress for both managers and employees alike.

Negative attitudes among employees often stem from the belief that those in authority do not care about their needs and desires. This belief is the result of inadequate communication. When lines of communication are damaged, anger and resentment build until nearly all statements and actions on both sides seem to damage the communication further. Negative beliefs reproduce themselves by coloring the interpretation of events no matter how neutral or positive they may seem to managers.

When the informal leaders of a group determine that the interests of their group are not going to be addressed, they mobilize the group as a whole to pressure those in authority to solve the problem. Ironically, the solutions they offer are rarely practical because the breakdown in communication prevents them from acquiring the information necessary to construct effective responses to the problems confronting them. Then, the attempt to force a solution to the problem by the informal leadership further disrupts communication when management reacts defensively. All too often, both sides resort to strategies aimed at domination through measures tainted with intimidation and manipulation.

So, exactly how can managers integrate the objectives of the informal organization with those of the company? The deceptively simple answer is to ask the employees as a group what their objectives are. Until management knows their objectives, they cannot integrate them with the company's objectives. Unfortunately, the employees themselves are almost never able to articulate their objectives because they haven't been formally developed and have very little to do with the objectives of the company. They are emotionally charged because their sole purpose is to satisfy the employees' social needs. Many of the employees' objectives are subliminal, and few are well formulated enough to be expressed without drawing a negative reaction from any manager who takes the time to listen.

Nevertheless, listening is the first step in the integration of organizational objectives. Skillful listening positively affects all organizational aspects of a company without further disruption of communication. In fact, it reduces the suspicion, anger, and negative attitudes of employees through a sort of emotional catharsis. Once the objectives of employees and the company have been integrated, continuous and frequent listening turns problems into creative and self-actualizing opportunities for both employees and managers to address jointly. Employees are free to cooperate, and they will police themselves through their informal organization. Those who do not cooperate with management will be pressured to do so by their peers.

Listening is a group activity that requires the participation of a manager and the employees constituting the target workgroup. Merely taking a survey or having employees place their concerns in a suggestion box and then reacting to the issues raised is not effective. The psychology of employees cannot be considered in isolation from the psychology of management.[93] It is clear that the actions and attitudes of management affect the actions and attitudes of employees. In addition, the interaction between managers and employees is continually affecting the interactions between the employees and managers. If management wants to integrate certain organizational objectives, they need to create an environment in which the employees feel free to speak with their managers without fear of retribution or disapproval.

It is critical for managers to realize that the facts of any situation in the workplace cannot be objectively determined. The views of employees and managers must be considered in their

---

93   Follett, "Relating: The Circular Response," *Mary Parker Follett Prophet of Management*, 46-48.

relation to each other at the same time. It is rare that any two people, whether manager or employee, will agree on the facts of any particular situation. Rational discussions aimed at convincing employees that they are wrong won't fare well because the meanings of the facts themselves are determined by the interactions between managers and employees. Employees often respond to the way messages are delivered just as strongly as to their content.

As far as employees are concerned, their interactions with managers have a dramatic effect on the meanings of facts and even the facts themselves. For this reason, managers do not have the luxury of addressing a single situation based on static facts. Any situation at any given time is evolving continually, with both the facts and their meaning changing. Reality is in a constant state of flux. Listening brings out the facts as employees view them and, in doing so, provides those who vent with an opportunity to examine those facts critically. Skillful listening is the first step toward the integration of organizational objectives because it allows managers to identify the issues that are important to employees. These issues cannot be addressed until they are known, and the process of identifying them heals many real and perceived grievances.

> **Managers can facilitate the identification of the real issues by listening proactively using the following method:**
> 1. Meet with the employees
> 2. Prime the group and ask for help
> 3. List the issues
> 4. Set a time to address the issues identified

1) Meet with the Employees

Before managers can make any significant progress toward managing the informal organizations that have evolved within their companies, they must first learn what their employees' real demands are. In the absence of an effective communication process, this is no easy task. The actual desires of employees are often obscured by the minor claims they raise and the ineffective way they present their demands.[94] Employees may not even be consciously aware of what is really troubling them in the work environment. They are simply responding emotionally to an environment that frustrates them. Remember, the informal organization is not based on logical reasoning; it does not plan, and it cannot directly articulate which needs are not being met because the employees who comprise the information organization are responding to the work environment emotionally.

Listening to a group of employees identify issues in the workplace brings their frustration into the open where it can be addressed. The very act of identifying frustrations and observing that the manager is interested enough to listen to them immediately reduces hostility and anger among the employees. The reason listening has this effect is that it engages employees in a rational activity while giving them an opportunity to express their anger in a civilized manner and in a calm setting. It allows them to air their grievances openly, and it creates the expectation that something will be done to address their concerns. However, until the employees identify those concerns and frustrations, neither they nor their managers can address them.

In human relations, it is never simply a case of the manager reacting to the employees. It is always more complex than that, and somewhat cyclical: The manager is actually reacting to the employees reacting to the manager. In turn, the employees react to the manager reacting to the employees. In other words, while

---

94   Follett, "Constructive Conflict," *Mary Parker Follett Prophet of Management*, 79.

each is trying to communicate with and influence the other, they are simultaneously reacting to each other's body language and word choice to determine the message being communicated. This process actually starts before the meeting begins.[95] This interaction is an essential part of the communication process because it allows everyone to adjust his or her opinions and attitudes based on the reactions and communications of others in the workgroup.

It is most effective to listen to the entire group at the same time because it constitutes the informal organization of the given workgroup. Communicating with the entire group gives the opportunity for high-status employees to have their say as the unofficial managers of the informal organization. Their participation lends credibility to the entire process. This is possible with workgroups consisting of around thirty employees or fewer. When workgroups are much larger, it becomes necessary to meet with representatives of the group to keep the size of the group manageable, and this entails the difficulty of selecting appropriate representatives for participation.

If the workgroup is so large that representatives must be used to keep the participants at a manageable number, high-status employees should be recruited for participation on the committee charged with identifying employee concerns. Their involvement will ensure that the employees who are unable to participate directly will view the work of the committee as legitimate. Employees with high status have the power to facilitate the acceptance and the integration of management objectives or to ensure the failure of such as just another attempt by management to manipulate the staff. If high-status employees participate in the process, they can be sure that the committee is not just an attempt by management to simply placate employees. Their power within the ranks of their coworkers ensures that the work of the committee will be accepted.

---

95 Follett, "Relating: The Circular Response," *Mary Parker Follett Prophet of Management*, 42-43.

Determining the high-status employees can be difficult because they have no official status within the formal organization, and they typically irritate their supervisors by being outspoken and critical of management. Recruiting employees who are favored by their supervisors as opposed to their peers is disastrous because the employee group from which they are selected will dismiss their work and opinions simply as a cynical ploy to win favor with management by participating in the manipulation. Management's flatterers are neither trusted nor respected by their coworkers. Although the participation of supportive employees may seem desirable to embattled managers, it is actually a detriment because it detracts from the legitimacy of the entire communication process.

Fortunately, locating high-status employees within workgroups is a relatively simple matter. Managers can simply ask the employees of the workgroup to choose their own representatives for the committee that will work on integrating organizational objectives. The employees know whom they respect, and they will select coworkers whom they believe will further their interests and stand up to management. Their chosen representatives are typically the spirited, opinionated, outspoken, and most vocal employees in the workgroup. They are usually the very employees the supervisors view as troublemakers.

In addition to those representatives chosen by the employees, managers should appoint a few technically adept employees to serve on the committee with them. Technically adept employees are those who have a high degree of expertise in the tasks of the workgroup based on their experience, education, or innate talent. These employees tend to do the work for the work's sake and take pride in their work. Their interest in the work itself adds an important dimension to the way in which the objectives ultimately are integrated. They provide important technical information during the communication process, and they contribute to the legitimacy of the entire process. Their presence is an indicator that management will take the work of the committee seriously.

Technically adept employees should be appointed to the committee by management in a ratio of about one employee selected by management to four selected by the workgroup. Any higher ratio raises the specter of manipulation. Once again, it is important to remember that ideally management should listen to the entire workgroup, and that committees should be used only when the workgroup exceeds thirty or so employees. However, when committees must be utilized due to the size of the workgroup, participation by high-status employees and a few technically adept employees is essential to the success of the communication process.

2) Prime the Group and Ask for Help

Before a group of employees will actively share their concerns, criticisms, and fears with managers, their natural reticence to reveal their feelings must be addressed. Employees will be concerned that what they say may hurt them in the future. To help overcome this, it is helpful for the manager to arrive early and welcome participants as they arrive. Once participants have been greeted and the meeting is convened, the manager should continue to break down the barriers to communication by priming the group. This is accomplished by acknowledging some of the issues to be discussed and listing them on chart paper. This helps members of the group move beyond their fear of the communication process to express their frustrations with the company.

Priming is accomplished by stating and listing the issues of which the manager is aware. The manager should then acknowledge that there are more issues and ask members of the group to assist in completing the list. This goes far in helping employees vocalize the issues that have been troubling them so that both the employees and management can address those issues and find solutions together. The more complete the list, the more effective this process will be in improving employee attitudes and increasing their support of the company. Nothing should be off limits.

Any matters that cannot be discussed will become precisely the issues that continue to fester beneath the surface and interfere with efficiency.

Consider, for example, a company in which the manager hears employees complaining about the favoritism of management toward certain employees and their lighter workloads. The manager is likely to deny the allegations of favoritism and defend the assigned workloads. When employees indicate that they are not convinced, it is natural for the frustrated manager to become angry with the employees. This reaction is immediately reinforcing for the manager because the employees stop complaining and retreat. Unfortunately, this has only driven their concerns underground where they will continue to grow and gather force. They will eventually resurface more powerfully or in other forms. When they do, it is very likely that the manager will again became defensive and drive them underground. This destructive cycle, unfortunately, is a downward spiral with each recurrence being more severe and complicated than the last.

If this manager decided to use the listening process described here to end the cycle, his previous responses to the expression of employee concerns would get in the way. His employees would have learned that when they express concerns, their manager becomes angry and their jobs are threatened. They would likely view the process as some sort of trick to identify ringleaders for termination of employment. Consequently, merely calling the group together and inviting the employees to comment on their problems will not generate much useful information. To overcome this natural reticence to participate, it is necessary for the manager to prime the pump by raising the most painful issues and opening them for discussion.

This is best done by standing before the group with chart paper and a marker in hand and explaining the purpose of the meeting. The manager simply thanks the employees for participating and informs them that the purpose of the meeting is to identify problems or issues that are of concern to the employees so that they can be addressed and solutions found. The manager then indicates that he is aware of at least two important issues, namely that he plays favorites and that workloads are unfairly distributed. He then lists both of these issues where everyone can see them. Following this, he asks employees to assist him in making a complete list of issues that need to be addressed. Seeing the manager list issues that he has previously denied or defended will free the participants to add to the list.

As issues are raised, it is critical that the manager simply record the issues without comment and thank the person for his or her courage in volunteering the information. When the manager raises a painful issue himself and lists it, he welcomes comment from employees and shows that he will not be defensive or angry. Managers can expect that some of the issues raised will be directed at them personally. Accepting these without anger or defensiveness goes very far in restoring the communication process and reducing employee anger.

When the manager listens to employees as a group, the employees do not merely respond to the manager's questions regarding employee frustrations. They also react to their own reactions to the activity. When a manager listens sincerely and without defensiveness, the emotional state of employees and their attitudes are affected. Employees' responses as they vent are actually a function of the interaction between themselves, the manager, and their peers as all react to one another simultaneously. They have an emotional experience that colors their perceptions of the company and frees them to evaluate their own ideas and attitudes. The process reduces anger, hostility, mistrust, and frustration while building hope and good will. Regardless of how critical the list of issues may appear, the employees themselves leave with more respect for their manager and greater trust in the motivations of management than they had prior to their participation in this activity.

A great deal of emotional energy is expended as employees vent to a manager who listens and does not become defensive. As the activity continues and the emotional tide recedes, the employees are free to consider problems more rationally. After the activity is completed, employees tend to lose interest in gossiping about problems because everything is in the open. If they raise a concern in private, other employees are likely to urge them to raise the issue with the manager directly. Furthermore, conversations tend to focus on what employees expect or hope management will do to address their issues. Management is viewed as sympathetic to employee concerns and a partner in improving the company.

3) List the Issues

After the group has been primed, and the manager has shown that the participants are free to share their concerns and frustrations, the participants will share a great deal in a very short time. All the manager needs to do is record the essence of the problems on the chart and thank each participant for volunteering the information. What is surprising to most managers employing this technique is that the matters raised are personal, emotional, and often based on misunderstandings and half-truths. The temptation for inexperienced managers who have not honed their listening skills is to restate the employees' concerns in an effort to "correct the facts for the record." This is a colossal mistake because it only increases hostility and mistrust. It is important to remember that emotions rather than facts are being addressed during the listening phase of the meeting. The time to address facts and perceptions will come much later in the integration process.

Because the process is emotionally charged, managers may become uncomfortable. It is almost a certainty that individual managers, management as a group, and official programs will be attacked. After all, employees typically see them as the source of their problems. But listening does not involve saving face or defending actions or positions. Refraining from making denials and defenses will ultimately change the tone of the meeting from one of confrontation to one of assisting management in identifying issues and problems important to everyone so that they can be addressed. Recording the issues where everyone can see them assures employees that their concerns are being taken seriously and their problems will be addressed.

Listing employee concerns and issues on large sheets of chart paper is convenient and works nicely with the processes that will follow. Writing with large, black markers in print approximately three inches tall assists in the readability of the concerns raised. In addition, the items in the list should be evenly spaced with no more than three to a page. The issues should not be numbered because they are not being prioritized. Prioritization of issues at this point only hinders the communication process. The utility of this will become apparent later when employees are requested to classify the issues. No attempt should be made to record exactly what is said. A few words that capture the essence of the problem are enough because the employees will have opportunities to elaborate and further define their concerns later. The listening process is a time to get everything out in the open as quickly as possible.

For example, an employee may volunteer the way the manager unfairly denies requests for time off. The manager knows that this employee is referring to a request in the past that the manager had no choice but to deny because of company policy. Although this was explained to the employee at the time, she still felt that it was unfair and that it was the manager's fault. Rather than remind the employee of this, the manager should simply write something such as *inconsistency in granting time off* on the chart and thank the employee for having the courage to raise the issue. This stops the group from being sidetracked by a discussion of company policy. The fact that the manager thanks the employee for volunteering this issue shows that he is not defensive and that it is safe to bring up any topic of concern. A manager who becomes defensive and attempts to set the record straight or explain his conduct will silence the group and ruin the process.

Each time a respondent raises an issue, the manager should thank him or her for the contribution and record it on the chart. This encourages others to participate, verifies the safety of the participants, and ensures the effectiveness of the process. Ultimately, it also increases trust and reduces hostility. It is crucial that the listening manager refrain from displaying anger or sarcasm. Each issue volunteered should be accepted as legitimate regardless of faulty assumptions, mistakes of fact, or apparent lies on which the issue is based. This is a time for managers to listen and record without reply.

When the manager is attacked with statements and questions such as, "You think we should…" or, "Tell us why you always make us…" the manager should identify the issues behind the statements by asking questions as necessary and list the issues behind the attacks without any type of defensive response. Instead, the manager should thank participants who volunteer issues for their courage, good will, and diligence. It is especially important to respond to attackers in this fashion.

For example, if an employee says, "Tell us why this company doesn't value us and treat us fairly," the manager should ignore the attack and respond simply by listing *company doesn't value us* and *company is unfair* on the chart. After listing these statements, the manager should ask the employee if he (the manager) has correctly ascertained the essence of the issues behind the employee's statement. If the employee volunteers more details, those should be recorded as well. After listing all the issues on the chart, the manager should thank the participant for his courage and candor in volunteering such painful issues. Under no circumstances should the manager attempt to answer the question posed because the employee is not really asking for information; he or she is making a statement of concern even though it is framed as a question.

Unfortunately, the skill of refraining from rebuttal is not natural for most people, and it may take practice for managers to acquire the ability to remain calm under fire. Managers who plan to listen to employee issues should be prepared to maintain their composure for the duration of the session. Venting sessions typically continue for about thirty minutes after the participants have been primed and only rarely last longer than this. Nevertheless, the issues identified will be valuable to management for future planning, and the process itself will release any hidden anger plaguing the company. Employees will leave cautiously hopeful and more supportive of their manager because he is apparently willing to listen and to do something about the problems they have identified.

4) Set a Time to Address the Issues Identified

When the group has exhausted its emotional energy and all of the issues they have raised have been listed, the manager should end this process by again thanking the participants for their help, bravery, and candor. It is important to end the activity by setting a time to meet again to begin addressing the issues and working toward solutions. Failure to set a time to meet is often interpreted as evidence that managers are merely stalling or, in the worst case, identifying ringleaders for adverse action such as demotion or termination. This can increase the hostility of the participants and foster perceptions of manipulation. In short, it can result in increasing the intransigence and dysfunction within the company.

When a date for further discussion is set following this process, the results can be surprising. Members of the group typically feel a little guilty for expressing frustration over issues that may seem minor in hindsight, and they regret being so tough on the manager. The non-defensive manager can expect to find allies among the participants who were not willing to come forward before the listening activity. The sense of hope that pervades the workgroup will have a positive impact on the functioning of the entire company. In fact, this effect is sometimes so profound that managers fail to continue with the process. Of course, failing to follow up on the listening activity is likely to lead to a loss of credibility and a resurgence of problems. Listening is only the first step in managing the informal organization of employees.

5) The Historical Foundation of Listening as a Strategy

In the 1930s, Elton Mayo noted that as company policies become more complex, managers must take greater pains to listen to the views of those who are charged with their implementation. He noted that it was imperative that employees understand the need for and ideas behind policies. Based on his experience at the Hawthorne plant, he recommended including interviews in the communication process to allow management to identify and effectively address what the workers themselves perceived as the real difficulties they were experiencing.[96] It was at the Hawthorne plant that Mayo first became aware of the power of listening to influence the attitudes and perceptions of employees.

In the early stages of Mayo's experiments, he thought that the employees involved performed better than the other employees because they enjoyed the attention of the researchers. However, as the years passed, the high output continued, and the employees reported that they did not feel pressured by management. In fact, they consistently cited the absence of pressure as their reason for preferring to work in the higher output "test room."[97] Some other variable had to be at work in maintaining the group's high achievement. That powerful, relatively permanent variable was the support of the employees' informal organization for meeting the objectives of the company. The listening performed by the researchers through the interview process was instrumental in securing that support, and the support remained after the interviewing had ceased.

---

96   Mayo, *The Human Problems of an Industrial Civilization*, 120.
97   Ibid., 71-72.

Managerial listening has a remarkable effect on the perceptions and attitudes of employees. This change manifests itself in the higher quality of communication between managers during departmental meetings. Employees who previously have been argumentative, suspicious, and legalistic become willing to cooperate with, place their trust in, and be supportive of management in resolving differences. Prior to listening, the informal organization of employees pressures its members to resist management. It does this through peer pressure and a negative interpretation of events. Once management is listening, all of this changes. The workgroup as a whole becomes supportive because management is interested in the employees and their problems. Employees are free to become part of the company's team.

The only way managers can discover their employees' attitudes and feelings toward the workplace is to listen to their employees, not just one time, but in an ongoing process of listening activities. When managers listen to employees for the first time, their comments are typically very brief expressions of anger and misinformation. However, the information gleaned is of the highest value to managers in reconciling the objectives of the employees with those of the company. Despite the recording of emotionally charged issues, managers typically leave the activity with a deeper understanding and concern for employees. This positively affects the way they work with their employees.

Mayo found that supervision improved almost simultaneously with the beginning of the listening process at the Hawthorne plant. Supervisors took a new interest in improving their supervisory methods. This went far in improving the performance of the entire workgroup. Management and employees were part of a team. It was evident almost from the outset that employees enjoyed the opportunity to express their ideas and that the supervisors themselves enjoyed listening.[98]

---

98   Ibid., 84.

Managers who listen without defensiveness or judgment realize that listening is an effective tool for creating a positive work environment, and they look forward to the communication process. They enjoy the power of being able to manage the informal organizations within their workgroups and do not find employee comments embarrassing or combative because they understand that they do not need to respond—they simply need to listen, and together they and their employees will work toward solutions.

In describing how employees respond, Mayo reported that the thoughts of some employees in the Hawthorne plant tended to gravitate toward a particular condition, event, or subject that completely overshadowed everything else. For others, several topics tended to predominate. In both situations, attempts to lead them to or away from what they wanted to share were unsuccessful.[99] Employees need to speak about the issues important to them and should not be led by the listening manager or instructed that specific topics are not open to discussion. Attempts to limit the communication process will only interfere with employees' attempts to bring their frustrations into the open where they can be managed.

Employees tend to choose topics of importance to their informal organization. If the manager asks questions or redirects employees' comments, the power of the activity is reduced or destroyed. Listening engages the informal organization by engaging its members in relevant discussions of important issues. The more skilled a manager is in conducting group listening, the more intimate the topics will be. Mayo found that listening actually modified the attitudes of the employees themselves.[100] The process of talking reveals new interpretations for employees and shifts their attitudes and beliefs. Listening reduces employee hostility toward management.

No advice, corrections, or solutions to problems should be offered by the manager during the listening process.[101] This would

---

99   Mayo, *The Human Problems of an Industrial Civilization*, 88-90.
100 Ibid., 90.
101 Ibid., 90-91.

immediately change the relation between the manager as listener and the employee as communicator. The employee perception that management will not listen and does not share employee interests will ultimately destroy the effectiveness of the communication process.

Even in situations where employees have a great number of grievances against their supervisors and are convinced that they have been treated unfairly, they will participate when they believe management is listening sincerely. They believe that the company will address their issues if only there is some way to communicate them.[102] Any attempt to justify, explain, or dispute a participant's view of the facts and problems during listening destroys this belief and is viewed as evidence that the activity is just another device used by management to manipulate and take advantage of employees.

Managers conducting listening activities often comment that what they hear is misinformed and inaccurate. Mayo observed this and noted that the information volunteered by employees was often lacking in objectivity. The facts and issues they shared were intimately bound up with the personal experiences and beliefs of the employees volunteering them.[103] He also noted that unfavorable comments tended to heavily outweigh the favorable during this stage of the process.[104] Managers should welcome unfavorable comments, however, because they are evidence that the issues being discussed among employees are also being shared honestly and openly with management.

The sharing of employee perceptions is the most important element of the listening activity. The statements volunteered by employees as they attempt to identify the issues they consider important are usually negative, angry, and fueled by self-interest. This reduces their usefulness as a secure basis for any action on the part of management. The listening being advocated here should not be thought of as a means of gathering facts. The information

---

102   Mayo, *The Human Problems of an Industrial Civilization*, 100.
103   Ibid., 92.
104   Ibid., 95.

shared by employees is useful to management only within the context of integrating the objectives of the informal organization with those of the company. At this stage, the sharing itself is the active ingredient in the process rather than what is being shared. It is the indispensible first step in the process of garnering the support of the informal organization.

What is being revealed is the attitude and emotional reaction of employees to the company. Listening in the sense described here is of use primarily in discovering the relations between management and employees.[105] Managers engaged in this process should not expect an accurate picture of objectively "real" conditions prevailing in the workplace. What they are sampling is the personality of the informal organization as expressed in its attitudes and beliefs. It is precisely these attitudes and beliefs that the listening process is designed to change and make more positive.

Managers who can listen without judgment will become aware of their employees' needs and challenges. This awareness dramatically improves their ability to motivate the people they supervise. Employees who can freely share their problems and opinions tend to feel that their supervisors are friends and allies rather than bosses. Their companies' successes become their successes, and their companies' challenges become their challenges. The come to understand that they share common interests and concerns with their companies.

Although it may seem to make more sense that employees would freely share their problems with their supervisors to improve understanding and make their jobs less difficult, most employees are naturally reticent to speak freely with managers. Employees typically resist attempts to discuss their problems with managers even when invited to do so. Employees expect their supervisors to judge rather than to sympathize with them or attempt to understand their situations. For this reason, they learn early on to hide their problems as well as any characteristics, actions, or

---

105   Mayo, *The Human Problems of an Industrial Civilization*, 101.

experiences that are likely to be different and, therefore, judged unfavorably. Instead, they attempt to defend their behavior by inventing explanations or excuses that they think will be acceptable to their coworkers and the manager.

Before employees can discuss their problems with their supervisors, they must be convinced that the listener/manager is genuinely attempting to gather information. Any defensiveness, attempts to correct facts or perceptions, or displays of anger or impatience casts managers in the role of judges and defeats the purpose of the listening activity.[106] Managers' body language while listening is just as important as their verbal responses are. Sincerity is indispensible.

When managers conduct a listening activity with their employees for the first time, they need to convince them that they are there to gather information rather than to judge or manipulate them. This is initially done by priming the participants with issues known by the manager to be controversial or troublesome. If the manager is willing to mention painful issues in front of the group, the participants will be more willing to share additional issues without fear of retaliation.

As a participant takes the risk and shares an issue during the listening activity, the manager's reaction will be critical in encouraging the other participants to risk bringing up their own concerns. Again, the manager must not be judgmental or defensive. After each employee shares a concern, the manager should list it for future reference and thank the employee for his or her candor in voicing the concern so that it can be addressed by the group. The manager's accepting manner and encouragement of participants will develop an atmosphere of trust and safety that will greatly increase the power of the activity to affect employee attitudes positively.

In the 1950s, Norman Maier discussed difficulties frequently encountered by managers when they attempt to implement their

---

106   Maier, Solem, and Maier, *Supervisory & Executive Development*, 240-243.

decisions with employees. When a directive is given to employees regarding a new procedure or duty, the employee may either accept it or reject it depending on the prevailing relationship between the informal organization and the company at the time. In effect, employees are invited to choose between doing something the old way or the new way each time they are directed by their managers to do something new.

When managers direct employees to make changes with relatively little explanation and limited discussion, they can expect distrust, fear, and hostility. These emotional responses are usually based on concerns that are imagined or unfounded and are not subject to logical refutation. Employees often perceive workplace changes as threats to their status and freedom within the informal organization. Managers soon learn that directly ordering employees to make changes based on management's prerogative rarely produces favorable results; thus, they are encouraged to rely on other methods for introducing change.

Another approach sometimes used by management in such situations is to attempt to sell employees on the new procedure or process. In selling an idea, managers attempt to communicate facts and rationales to employees in an effort to convince them that the change is necessary and desirable. Unfortunately, significant experimental evidence proves that this approach is not very effective in reducing resistance to change among employees.[107] The problem is that it relies on management-directed communication rather than on listening to employees.

A third approach, which is more effective because listening plays a greater role, is a problem-solving approach that involves presenting the facts to the group and asking them to identify a solution. When this approach is used, members of the workgroup typically identify a number of possible solutions. It is more effective because the solutions offered take the feelings and needs of

---

107   Ibid., 96-98.

the employees into account. Employees feel a sense of ownership and importance in making their solution successful.

When the employees identify solutions, resistance is greatly reduced because they tend not to fear decisions they make themselves. By way of contrast, selling techniques can often actually increase fears stemming from feelings of being manipulated or railroaded by management. Problem-solving approaches go further than merely allowing employees to voice their objections. They allow them to be involved in the solutions to the problems facing the company.

The difficulty with giving employees the freedom to solve problems in the name of participative management is that they may lack the necessary expertise to arrive at a workable solution, and the objectives of their informal organization may be different or even inconsistent with those of the company. None of these approaches is ideal, and each of them raises difficulties for management. In practice, there are times when each of these approaches may be appropriate, but management can expect to encounter difficulties anytime changes need to be made. Even when successful, they do not permanently affect informal organizations. Managers using them are compelled to take the most prudent course available and deal with the undesirable consequences as they arise.

An alternative to reliance on these strategies lies in developing a communication process that permanently alters employee-management interactions. Ongoing communication allows the informal organization to be managed on a permanent basis. This first step in developing this communication process is effectively listening.

Employees do not become interested in facts until they have processed their fears and hostilities by expressing them. Only then are they free to gather facts and begin a problem-solving process that integrates their interests with those of the company.[108] The

---

108   Ibid., 190.

very expression of their perceptions stimulates employees to question their facts, emotions, and thinking.

The process of expression makes it possible for employees to work with management in making identified solutions to problems workable. A cooperative, well-managed informal organization will support solutions that it views as consistent with its objectives even in the absence of significant employee participation in the development of those solutions. Effective management of the informal organization beginning with skillful listening will make nearly any approach the company takes to address changing circumstances successful.

The effectiveness of the listening process is significantly determined by the attitude of the manager using it. Resistance to managerial attempts to address problems in the workplace is almost certain if the manager complains about employee motivations or performance or has a critical attitude toward those she supervises.[109] Stating that the problems are the employees' fault will only produce defensiveness and hostility, both of which are not conducive to communication or cooperation.

If the manager's attitude is one of helpful interest in improving conditions for employees or making their jobs easier, the employees will respond with cooperation and support. This positive attitude must be expressed during the listening activity and thereafter if the support of the informal organization is to be won. Sincere listening without judgment or defensiveness expresses genuine, benign interest and forms the basis for future cooperation. Effectively utilizing the informal organization within a company resolves patterns of conflicting forces that escape objective quantification and evaluation.[110]

While engaging employees in a discussion prior to making decisions can be advantageous, conducting discussions in all cases isn't practicable. Consider a situation in which a manager needs

---

109 Maier, Solem, and Maier, *Supervisory & Executive Development*, 274.
110 Ibid., 66-67.

to make a decision without input. Obtaining employee acceptance after the fact can be challenging. In such a situation, the manager can meet with subordinates, inform them of the decision and its rationale, and then ask for their input. Utilizing the listening technique allows the manager to determine whether the employees consider the decision acceptable. If the employees accept the decision, the manager can implement it immediately.

If the employees oppose the decision, the manager can engage the employees in identifying the issues it raised and determine whether to proceed and work out the problems as they arise, or postpone implementation until the idea can be processed at length with the employees. Where opposition is significant, a modest delay in implementation is preferable to the risk of sabotage. In either circumstance, listening is critical to the alignment process in which the objectives of the informal organization are integrated with those of the company.

Listening is also useful in situations in which a manager, having made a decision, takes time to discuss the best way to implement it with subordinates. If the implementation of the decision can occur in various ways, and it makes relatively little difference which alternative is chosen, employees are afforded a significant opportunity for input. Listening becomes important in the ensuing discussions regarding evaluation of the implementation method chosen. Asking employees to identify problems facilitates optimization of the implementation process and goes far in maintaining integration of employee and company objectives.

If a manager is in a position to allow even more employee participation, the discussion of a pending decision could be undertaken with employees before finalizing it. In this situation, employee input becomes a vital part of the decision. This typically results in greater acceptability of the decision. Listening is important here both during the decision making process and the implementation process. Listening promotes the ongoing support of employees and ensures the maximum level of cooperation.

Ongoing listening establishes that the manager is interested in the welfare of the employees and the company.

Employee participation in decision-making processes fulfills their self-actualizing needs and develops the ability to accept responsibility for the successes and failures of the company. The degree of employee participation will vary depending on the nature of the decisions made. In addition, employee interest will vary. Some members of a workgroup will view certain matters as highly significant, whereas others will consider them trivial. Regardless of the level of participation, employee support can be maintained through an ongoing communication process in which listening plays a crucial role.

The need for employee involvement may vary depending on the importance of the issue. It is not easy for managers to know the difference beforehand because of the emotional rather than rational grounding of informal organizations. All significant managerial action involves the risk that situations may unexpectedly become emotionally charged. When this occurs, and it does occur with some regularity in most companies, holding discussions in which employees are invited to identify the issues troubling them reduces or eliminates hostility. If management ignores the employees' reaction to managerial decisions, organizational effectiveness will decrease.

Some managers fear that if employees are given the opportunity to participate in the decision-making process, they will demand input in matters that need to be exclusively within the purview of management. These managers avoid listening because they worry that they may not be able to meet employee demands or solve the problems employees raise in their discussions. The experience of managers who allow employee participation and who conduct regular listening activities has not supported these fears.[111] Employee demands for control do not increase with participation, and they do not expect managers to solve every prob-

---

111   McGregor, *The Human Side of Enterprise*, 172-173.

lem or accede to every request. Managers who master listening skills tend to change their attitudes and become increasingly open to employee input. Listening actually broadens management's conception of the issues that concern employees, and it increases mutual support within the company.

Limiting discussions to objective conditions as opposed to less tangible emotional issues is not a successful strategy. Managers concerned with their inability to handle employee anger and demands for unreasonable managerial action sometimes preface discussions by listing topics that are off the table or non-negotiable. When managers fail to listen to concerns regarding relatively intangible issues in the workplace, employees will express their hostility in other ways.[112] For example, they may file formal grievances over issues that are tangible but relatively unimportant to them because this is the only way they can be heard. Despite the cost to the company in terms of both time and money, however, the real problems are never addressed.

Consider a situation in which employees suddenly begin to bring a series of relatively trivial grievances to management involving wages, hours, and working conditions. The apparent new and widespread dissatisfaction may be a symptom of deeper problems. The way to address this is to conduct a listening activity in which the employees feel free to express their private feelings without risking managerial disapproval or retribution. The underlying problems usually have little or nothing to do with the issues on which the formal grievances are grounded. Addressing the underlying issues is impossible as long as management is unaware of their nature. In many instances, the issues simply evaporate once employees feel that someone has listened to them.

During the listening activity, it is common to discover that the actual concerns of the employees stem from how their supervisor treats them or speaks to them rather than any of the issues raised formally. Since they recognize, at least subconsciously, that they

---

112   McGregor, *The Human Side of Enterprise*, 189.

will not be taken seriously by raising the intangible characteristics of their supervisor's behavior, they express their anger and discontent by grieving tangible issues. Listening very often takes care of the problem without the necessity of further processing. Until the manager gives the employees the opportunity to express their dissatisfaction, they will continue to look for ways to get even through grieving trivial policy violations, soldiering, or sabotage.

In the 1980s, Philip Crosby commented on what he called hassling within companies. Hassling consists of ongoing, low profile arguing, fighting, and sabotage. Hassling in the workplace cannot be prevented on a case-by-case basis. Instead, managers and employees need to learn to communicate. Hassling is expensive and wasteful because hassled people produce low quality work, and, in some situations they do little work at all.

Crosby defined "hassle companies" as those in which management and employees are at odds. In hassle-free companies, all employees work together with management, and neither group takes sides.[113] Hassle-free companies provide pleasant working relationships, smooth processes and systems, and happy employees. Their environments facilitate the potential for maximum profits and growth. Both employees and customers feel confident in companies of this sort. In hassle companies, employees spend more energy interfering with each other than they do working. Much effort is spent evening the score among employees and managers as they attempt to work within damaged interpersonal relationships. Disruption is largely an inside job brought about by the very people doing the work.

The employees themselves generate tasks for each other that are wholly unrelated to their jobs or the missions of their departments and companies. The employees creating these hassles do so without purpose or malicious intent. They are simply reacting to the seemingly insignificant day-to-day push and shove within their companies. The difference between hassle and hassle-free

---

113 Crosby, *Quality without Tears: The Art of Hassle-Free Management*, 19.

companies rests for the most part in attitude and communication practices. Listening is used frequently in hassle-free companies to assuage hostility and eliminate unproductive work.

Again, managerial listening is difficult in practice because managers tend to fear that once employees have brought problems into the open, their solutions become the responsibility of management. This raises the specters of additional work, unfavorable reactions from senior management, unexpected and unreasonable costs, and loss of face. To use the listening technique at all, managers must understand that listening is only the first step in a process in which employees rather than management have an opportunity to address their problems. The process ultimately results in employees taking upon themselves the ownership of the real problems they face.

When the problems addressed through the informal organization cannot be solved, they are redefined or accepted as conditions that are not amenable to change. It is the process of acknowledging problems, taking ownership of them, and working through them that aligns the objectives of the informal organization of employees with those of the company—not the actual, objective solution of the problems identified. The first step in the process is identifying what the real problems are through skillful, non-defensive, and non-judgmental listening.

6.

DEVELOPING RELEVANT GOALS

Once the real issues facing employees are identified, it is possible to address them. Unknown, suppressed problems cannot be solved. A key aspect of the process of improving employee attitudes and increasing their support for the objectives of management is to transfer ownership of the problems to those with the power to solve them—the employees themselves. This begins when the manager has the employees develop one or more goals to address each issue raised during listening activities. Redirecting anger, fear, and dissatisfaction into achievable goals also redirects the energy of the entire informal organization of employees. A long list of negative conditions and issues becomes a positive statement of what can be done to reach the potential of the employees and the company.

Changing complaints or problems into goals depersonalizes negative statements and allows the participants to focus on the problems rather than each other and their managers. This greatly reduces anger in the work environment by introducing a new element of hope. Redirecting the negative focus of informal organizations opens new opportunities for cooperation between managers and employees in addressing mutual concerns. Employees who participate in rewriting issues as goals feel that management has listened to them and cares about their contribution to the company.

Since the objectives of the company are not those of the informal organization of employees, listening is essential to the determination of employee concerns, attitudes, and priorities. Taking the time to allow employees to rewrite the issues they identify as goals is crucial to the alignment of organizational objectives. While nearly all of the issues raised by employees during listening will be negative and emotionally charged, goals are of necessity positive in nature because they are desirable outcomes. Employees buy into these goals because they created them.

Merely having managers develop goals from the issues raised by employees is ineffective because it deprives employees of participation in the process. When managers develop the goals, it becomes the task of management to meet them. Employees feel little or no ownership of those goals and thus take no responsibility for achieving them. The process will become yet another example of the ineffectiveness of management. Developing goals in concert with employees promotes the resolution of negative emotions and provides opportunities for employees to satisfy their needs relating to status, acceptance, and respect.

In addition, managers who attempt to develop goals from the issues raised by their subordinates soon learn that the task is for the most part impossible. The issues raised are very often negative expressions of emotions arising from faulty understanding and erroneous data. Managers who fall into this trap naturally tend to feel that perceptions and errors need to be corrected before any useful goal can be identified. Unfortunately, attempts on the part of management to correct these misperceptions are interpreted as defensiveness by employees. Only the employees themselves can correct their misperceptions.

Furthermore, the employees themselves must revisit their data, perceptions, conclusions, and attitudes if their informal organization is to be managed. The process of converting issues into goals does just this. It allows employees to define their problems by determining what specifically needs to be done to eliminate them. Employees view goals they have developed themselves as relevant and legitimate. For this reason, they are more inclined to take responsibility for their accomplishment and tend not to hold management responsible if the goals are not attained.

When employee goals are integrated with or made consistent with the formal goals of management, the informal organization of employees becomes supportive of management. When the relationship between the company and its informal organizations is disturbed due to changing circumstances, the company cannot assume it has the support of the informal organization. Listening goes far in determining the level of acceptability of managerial strategies, and employee goal setting harnesses the support of their informal organization.

Any sort of change, regardless of how insignificant it may seem to management, can be perceived threatening by employees. Even changes that seem to generate relatively small threats to their interests may have a significant cumulative effect on morale. When a workgroup has developed hostility based on a few, specific issues, it is very common for its counterproductive emotions to generalize to other situations and people who are not involved at all. This further complicates any direct approaches management takes to deal with the issues. The employees often cannot articulate the most important issues without processing their emotional reactions to the workplace.

For this reason, the issues identified by employees cannot serve as a basis for the development of goals by managers. Many of the most important issues will be understated with less important issues being overstated. At this stage of the process, employees frequently raise issues that are mostly irrelevant to the real problems of the workgroup. They include them to express their anger and to emphasize how difficult their situation has become. Dealing with these red herrings wastes limited resources and frustrates managers who often express the feeling that they can't do anything right, and that nothing will satisfy the employees.

When employees convert the issues into goals, they further define their views of the problems they face. The actual importance of the various issues troubling them is then evaluated critically. During the process of goal identification, employees sometimes redefine their problems to the point that the goals they develop can scarcely be traced back to the issues that generated them. Relatively unimportant issues are subsumed under broadly stated goals and thus are ignored. The goal development process counteracts this by dramatically improving everyone's focus and keeping it on the real issues at hand.

Engaging the informal leadership is a critical step in group problem-solving and change processes. Identifying goals that will address unacceptable conditions engages members of the group and tends to develop a positive common purpose among members and management. The energy of groups properly engaged in goal setting is directed toward the positive end of improving negative situations rather than punishing those responsible for them. It helps members of the group to accept ownership of the problems, and it empowers them to actively solve them. The desire for revenge arising from anger is replaced with enthusiasm for improvements arising from newfound hope. Changes are viewed as positive steps toward a brighter future.

The people who set goals aimed at solving problems come to own both the problems and their solutions. As long as management is viewed as owning the problems, it is natural for employees to resent managers for not solving them. Goal identification begins the process of delivering the ownership of company problems to the employees—the only personnel capable of solving them. It moves the focus of employee discussions away from blaming managers for difficulties toward identifying changes that will benefit both the employees and the company. In instances in which management is viewed as the problem, effective goal setting by employees harnesses the power of the informal organization to increase good will and improve interpersonal relations.

Managers can facilitate employee goal setting by following three steps:
1. Review the issues.
2. Categorize concerns.
3. Develop goals.

1) Review the Issues

The group listening technique produces a comprehensive list of issues relevant to employees and their informal organization as a whole. Reviewing the issues and problems identified is evidence that the manager took the employees seriously, listened sincerely, and is interested in them. The employees do not feel that their problems have been swept under the table or that management was only attempting to manipulate or pacify them. The very act of reading and reviewing the list of issues increases trust and breaks down the barrier between employees and management. Hostile postures of us versus them diminish because management is openly acknowledging the existence of the issues identified by the employees.

2) Categorize Concerns

After reading and reviewing the issues the employees have identified, the manager begins the process of giving the workgroup ownership for the problems identified. This is important because only the employees have the power to actually deal with issues in their informal organization. Because the issues are emotionally rather than rationally based for the most part, they are not amenable to direct intervention on the part of management. In addition, as employees' objectives are brought into alignment with those of the company during the problem-solving process, they are better able to redefine the issues they perceive as problematic.

Managers who believe that all that is desired is a solution to a problem are quite mistaken and often frustrated when their quick fixes are not applauded by their employees. They fail to grasp that employees are able to meet their social needs only through participating in the problem solving process. When employees develop their own goals, they will accept ownership of both successes and failures to attain them. Often, the problems most relevant to the informal organization of employees are not as important to management because they have only minimal impact on operations.

In the absence of listening and goal development activities that involve the workgroup directly, managers are often misled regarding what issues are most significant. This occurs because employees tend to work around their real concerns by focusing on problems that should at least be legitimate to management. As the process progresses and trust levels increase among employees, they redefine problems significantly.

Issues will shift and focus as employees come to see the relationships between issues and group them together. A convenient technique for facilitating the classification of issues by employees is simply to cut the previously recorded issues from the chart paper on which they were listed and distribute them among the participants so that similar issues can be grouped together. Large groups of participants can be divided into subgroups of five or six to make the work of the group more efficient. If this is done, the manager can simply read the issues on the slips and ask which subgroup would like to work on solutions for that type of issue.

Once all of the issue papers have been distributed, the manager can ask the participants to identify a common heading or name for the categories of issues they have been assigned. The result is that each subgroup has a number of categories of issues for which they will develop goals to address the issues. The goals developed should be positive, generalized statements of what employees believe would solve the problems they face. However, management should be receptive of all participants' ideas .

It is not important or desirable for the manager to determine which goals are reasonable or practical. Any attempt to do this will deprive the employees of ownership and thereby reduce the effectiveness of the activity. This hands-off tactic is difficult for managers inexperienced in problem solving with informal organizations because they worry that they are creating false expectations and will not be able to meet employee demands.

It is important for management to remember that the goals identified by employees ultimately will belong to them along with the responsibility for attaining them. Sharing this reality with the participants at this stage, however, is ill advised because it can discourage the employees and interfere with the process before they have sufficiently defined their desires and taken ownership of their problems. Ultimately, managers will assume the role of helpful partners rather than omnipotent and misdirected problem solvers when employees begin to address their problems.

3) Develop Goals

When the participants have grouped related issues together, they are ready to develop goals to address each issue. While formulating the goals without the interference of management, employees begin to take ownership of the process as well as the problems they have identified. Developing goals requires the employees to further define their frustrations and determine what they actually want. In this manner, goal development moves the focus from complaining and venting to identifying problems and working toward solutions. This is indispensible to securing the support of the informal organization. The real goals of employees cannot be integrated with those of the company until the employees and management are specifically aware of them.

Positive statements of desirable outcomes introduce an element of hope and inspire employees with a willingness to reexamine their objectives for the purpose of refining and improving them. The move from painstakingly identifying every undesirable aspect of the workplace to positively stating what would make it more pleasant and efficient is exciting and motivating for employees because participation meets some of their self-actualizing needs. Managers do not need to be concerned with whether the specific goals identified can be met. Participation in the process of developing goals as opposed to the literal attainment of them improves employee attitudes

At the end of this process, the goals developed by subcommittees of five or six employees need to be reviewed by the entire group to ensure their legitimacy. This allows the manager and the participants to acknowledge one another for the hard work involved in developing the goals. It affirms the importance of the work to the company and satisfies the employees' needs to be taken seriously, to accomplish important tasks, and to exert significant influence on their work environment.

It cannot be over emphasized that employees must do this work themselves if the process is to be effective in increasing the level of support of their informal organization. Presenting goals developed by management and merely asking a group of employees for their endorsement will not be successful in improving employee attitudes or in engaging a resistant informal organization.

When managers find themselves compelled to present goals for a workgroup that they alone have developed, they should present them openly and take responsibility for them. They should never attempt to convince employees that the goals are really employee goals. It's much more effective to present management's goals as such and ask employees to help identify the issues that need to be addressed to meet them. This can be accomplished by revisiting listening activities and goal-setting processes to engage the informal organization of employees. When managers listen to employees as they identify the issues raised by their directives and develop goals to address them, they are actually engaging the informal organization in the integration of employee interests with those of management. The listening and goal-setting processes are important strategies in the implementation of strategic plans.

4) The Historical Foundation of Goal Setting as a Process

In the 1920s, Mary Parker Follett recognized that employees are not always aware of what the real issues are for them and neither is management. The most emotional and high profile problems do not always indicate the issues actually involved. Most situations in the workplace are complex and involve numerous and overlapping interactions. Managers often tend to react to the most dramatic issues without realizing that those may not be the most significant issues to the employees.[114]

Follett encouraged managers to search for the real sources of conflict between employees and managers. The issues initially raised by employees are often only symbolic of the real issues. Attempts to address those issues will waste energy and resources because the real issues will not be addressed. While listening allows employees to bring the real conflict out into the open, their demands and complaints are often only symbols of the real issues. Goal setting provides employees with an opportunity to further examine and define the issues that matter to them once they have been brought to light.

For example, consider a situation in which management wants to introduce new machines in a plant. The manager takes the time to explain to the operators that the new machinery is more efficient and safer than what they are using. Due to technical requirements for the machinery, it will need to be placed in a different location in the plant. Operators will receive small increases in their hourly rate and be trained to operate the new equipment.

---

114   Follett, "Constructive Conflict," *Mary Parker Follett Prophet of Management*, 77.

While this seems to be nothing but good news, the manager is surprised when the operators do not welcome these changes. When asked why, they inform the manager that the old equipment is good enough for them, and they are happy where they are. They further state that the small increase in wages does not adequately compensate them for the difficult job of learning how to operate the new machinery.

When the machinery is finally installed and placed in operation, the operators continue to complain and ultimately file grievances regarding the temperature in the area and questionable violations of company policy by the manager. While the temperature is only a few degrees different from what it was at the previous location, it does present a somewhat legitimate complaint that must be addressed through the grievance procedure. Of course, technical violations of company policies typically carry the color of legitimacy and increase the manager's stress.

In an attempt to deal with the situation, the manager seeks to prove to the operators that the temperature in the new area is within acceptable limits and that company policies have not been violated. Without creating an opportunity for the operators to vent, the manager does not listen to the issues they volunteer; therefore, the only source of information the manager has is what employees tell him individually, and this information is not complete. The manager finds himself on the defensive in a hostile workplace.

Without engaging in the listening process, the manager will not learn that the temperature issues and policy violations were raised only because they were at least legitimate complaints, and as such, the employees knew they wouldn't be reprimanded for raising them. If the manager had provided an opportunity for venting, he would have learned that the problem had more to do with the location of the new machines than with the temperature in that area of the plant, and thus the alleged policy violations were not of any real importance to the employees at all. By allowing the operators to engage in goal setting, he might have further learned that what the operators were actually concerned about was their status among their coworkers within the plant.

In this plant, the employees assigned to the new machines were chosen based on their seniority. The proximity of the old machines to the break room increased free time during breaks, and because of this benefit, the operators of those machines were considered the "in crowd" by the other workers. Even though the increased length of free time may have been nominal, the perceived higher status of the operators was powerful enough to affect their attitudes and willingness to cooperate with the manager.

The problem of the distance of the machines from the break room is a totally different problem from what the manager spent his time addressing—the temperature in the new area of the plant and the technical interpretation of company policies. Even if the temperature issues were met and legal wrangling had shown that there had been no policy violations, new issues could be expected to emerge in the future because the real problem had nothing to do with temperature. It had to do with status, and the old machines had become symbols of that status for their operators.

It is very likely that even if the manager had conducted listening activities, the employees would not have spoken about this perceived issue of status. Instead, the issue was more likely to emerge as one regarding the distance to the break room. If the manager attempted to act on the issues identified during direct listening, he may have wrongly concluded that the employees were demanding that the break room be moved closer to them. However, if he had allowed the employees to further define the problem during goal development exercises, he would have learned that the employees would be satisfied with a nominal amount of increased break time. Changing or refusing to change the location of the break room would have only further impaired morale.

This scenario is an example of how allowing employees to define their goals allows them to reformulate their symbols and protect their status. Grappling with the issues of the length of break time and the location of the break room during goal setting would provide the operators with an opportunity to determine just what they really wanted and ultimately recognize that the temperature and technical policy violations were not serious issues. They were only symbols of their status within the plant. Through the goal setting process, the operators would confront their true desires and make management aware of them for the first time.

During goal setting, the operators are likely to have addressed the length of their breaks in light of their new location. In addition, they may have suggested the introduction of experience requirements for becoming operators of the new machinery as a safety measure. While neither of these suggestions may seem to have much to do with status to the manager, it should be remembered that employees create their own status symbols and the rationales for them as they work through the process.

If the length of break time was slightly increased at the request of the operators, their status among their coworkers would increase because management responded to their request. This in conjunction with their suggestions regarding the new experience requirements for becoming operators would go far to safeguard their status within the plant, and the new equipment would gain value as symbolic of that status. If management had unilaterally increased the break times or imposed the experience requirements, the employees' status would not have been preserved.

In this example, the loss of a status symbol was the cause of employee dissatisfaction. In the absence of processes to engage employees in working on their own problems, the degree of employee cooperation cannot be increased. Without listening to employees and allowing them to set goals, managers are severely limited in their ability to deal with the often symbolic concerns of employees because they cannot discover what those concerns are or identify effective strategies for addressing them.

Managers would do well to remember that what employees perceive as ends are often the means to other, more significant ends.[115] Consider for example a company that fabricates doors used in residential and commercial construction. Most employees are not interested in the official purpose of the company per se, which is to provide contractors with reliable components and to make a profit for the shareholders.

While work meets a number of needs for employees, the importance of these needs varies from employee to employee. Some employees are primarily concerned with the income their jobs provide. Others may also value their jobs as a way to gain the experience necessary to enhance their careers. Regardless of the income their jobs provide, nearly all employees also want their jobs to be sources of status, and they want the satisfaction of their work needs to be taken seriously.

While all employees need the income they earn, they will respond to incentives and the directives of management differently depending on their individual values and relative priorities. Their desires are largely subconscious and emotionally based. Goal setting brings their priorities out into the open and allows them to be scrutinized and aligned with the goals of other employees and with the company.

The process itself generates group purposes and the rationales for them. Follett tells the story of a few citizens of a New England town who decided that they needed a social welfare department. The inhabitants of the town didn't know what it was or what purpose it would serve. Nevertheless, a small group of citizens made the suggestion and garnered enough support that the department was organized.

After it was organized, the townspeople told each other, as well as people in neighboring towns, what their purpose had been in organizing their social welfare department. Although they had no idea what the department would do, it appeared to the townspeople, and to those they spoke to, that they had wanted and needed

---

115   Follett, "Relating: The Circular Response," *Mary Parker Follett Prophet of Management*, 58.

the department for a considerable time prior to organizing it.[116] In short, the people of the town developed their rationale for the purpose of the department as they organized it and developed goals for it. The interesting this here is that rationales were developed as the townspeople set goals together.

The same principle is at work when employees set goals. The process itself tends to define, clarify, and provide a rational basis for the needs that the goals will meet. Unmet needs that were previously emotional and largely unexpressed become sufficiently defined to be met within the workplace. It's no wonder that managers often find the machinations of informal organizations perplexing in the absence of listening to their employees' concerns and engaging in goal-setting processes with them. Only when the employees themselves have clarified their goals and priorities can those be integrated with those of the company.

In the 1940s, Chester Barnard noted that people are universally active and seek purposes for their activity. Recurring social contact without some purpose or activity is generally impossible.[117] People feel compelled to do something when they are together. The enduring existence of any business organization depends on its employees deriving satisfaction from their interpersonal interactions in the workplace.

The objectives of informal organizations may appear to be trivial, but they influence nearly every employee in the company. In fact, it may make little difference whether employee goals are accomplished or not. Individually, employees may even be indifferent toward many of the conditions they address as a group. The goal-setting process itself is the active agent that facilitates interactions leading to socially desirable association, cooperation, and conversation among employees and managers. The goal identification process engages the informal organization through communication.

---

116   Ibid., 59.
117   Barnard, *The Functions of the Executive*, 118.

The need for the informal organization to be involved in something is similar to the needs of people to have outlets for activity involving association with others. When a person is unemployed, he often find himself in a social vacuum that produces a feeling of being lost. Barnard reported that when a number of people experience this, they are likely to do any sort of "mad thing."[118] In fact, they are almost driven to it. Attempts to curtail the natural operation of informal organizations of employees often result in unexpected, negative consequences for management. Workers have a need to interact within groups of their peers. The relation of employees to their companies is through those with whom they have direct contact.[119] Social interaction requires one on one contact. The relationships employees have with each other are much more significant to them than their loyalty to the company for which they work.

Oftentimes, the willingness of employees to endure inadequate wages, hours, and working conditions can be explained by their need to maintain some sense of social integration with their peers. Goal setting provides this interaction and directs the energy of employees toward the positive purpose of improving the workplace by integrating the objectives of the company with their own. The process of goal setting fulfills the employees' self-actualizing needs.

In the 1950s, Norman Maier observed that success in problem solving in the workplace is largely dependent on management's failure to provide solutions for every problem that arises.[120] Employees need to own and address problems themselves. They do not want to work for all-knowing, all-powerful managers. They want to play a significant role in problem solving. It is actually desirable for managers to admit that they are unaware of problems when employees bring them to their attention for the first time.

---

118   Ibid., 118.
119   Ibid., 118-119.
120   Maier, Solem, and Maier, *Supervisory & Executive Development*, 66-67.

This allows them to avoid taking sides and showing preferences for particular solutions.

Since many problems involve status within the informal organization, allowing employees to address their own issues through goal setting typically provides more efficient solutions to problems than managers are ever likely to stumble upon on their own. Managerial attempts at problem solving often fail because they deal with objective conditions rather than the emotional symbolism of the informal organization. In addition, solutions to problems devised by management are not as satisfying to employees as those they arrive at on their own.

Norman Maier observed that problem-solving methods that place managers in helpful rather than authoritative roles have significant advantages over those in which managers dictate solutions.[121] Even managers with minimal skills can obtain high-quality solutions to problems in the workplace when they take a democratic approach that includes employees in goal development. Employees support their own goals and ensure the success of efforts to meet them.

Engaging employees in the development of goals aimed at solving their problems improves the thinking of both the employees and managers beyond anything they might deduce in the absence of this process. Employees tend to enthusiastically accept solutions developed through the goal-setting process because they developed and addressed the issues that were relevant to them. The development of goals is the first step toward the rationalization of emotional issues that tend to predominate among employees.

One of the most frequently used approaches to motivating employees to work toward goals developed by management involves the use of incentives and disincentives. This often boils down to motivating employees through their fear of losing the incentives or being penalized if goals are not supported. One of the shortcomings of this approach is that it places supervisors in

---

121   Ibid., 276.

the roles of being spies or enforcers.[122] They become the enemy rather than a resource or team member.

If that were not enough, fear-based motivators encourage cheating by employees. When this occurs, the burden on managers to be even more vigilant is increased, and the motivation to meet goals promptly breaks down in the manager's absence. For example, penalties imposed on employees who fail to work toward management's safety goals can have the undesirable effects of encouraging them to falsify the data on accident reports and follow safety procedures only when managers are present to enforce them.

Employees working toward their own goals do not need outside authority or financial incentives. Their managers are not spies or enforcers. Instead, they are working partners who can provide technical expertise, training, and resources to assist employees in their quest to improve their workplace while pursuing the objectives of the company. Company problems become the common enemy of both employees and managers.

Incentives and disincentives are also ineffective because goals set by the employees themselves are typically more exacting and strict than management could successfully request or demand.[123] Employees are more willing to take chances and work toward loftier objectives when they set their own goals because they don't fear the consequences of failure. When management sets goals, employees worry about what the future will hold for them. For example, will the expectations of management regarding their performance be unreasonably increased? Will they lose their jobs or be demoted if they fail to reach their goals? Employee goal setting frees employees to reevaluate and overcome what they otherwise might perceive as their limitations. The goal-setting process largely eliminates employees' fear of change.

---

122   Ibid., 99-100.
123   Ibid., 190.

Douglas McGregor writing in the 1960s noted the importance of employees accepting responsibility for goals. When employees are committed to attaining goals, they are self-directed and self-motivated.[124] People are only rarely committed to working toward objectives developed and imposed externally by management. When employees are directed to pursue company goals, they typically only accept them passively, which usually leads to apathy and hostility toward management. To combat this, employee involvement in goal setting is necessary to managerial planning. Managers should not be concerned if they believe that goals set by employees are unrealistic or too high.

Unattainable goals will be redefined or abandoned by the informal organization while employee support of company objectives will continue undiminished. The goals of the informal organization are typically emotional and aimed at meeting employees' self-actualizing needs regardless of how they're framed. The process of developing goals and working toward them meets these needs. When employees participate in the goal-setting process, their objectives and those of the company are integrated. They will view company objectives as having priority over their own objectives. After all, the informal organization would cease to exist in the absence of its successful formal organization—the company.

McGregor found this to be the case in the Scanlon Plan companies.[125] Although there were emotional disagreements, the problems mainly had to do with improving efficiency—a company objective. This was the case because individual employees had a stake in the success of their company. Their personal goals and objectives had been successfully integrated with those of management. The success of the company was identified with the success of the employees.

This could not be adequately explained by the economic incentives provided by management alone. Employees were genuinely

---

124   McGregor, *The Human Side of Enterprise*, 94-95.
125   Ibid., 157-158.

committed to company goals because their satisfaction was intimately bound up with the success of their company. Pursuing company goals was the best way for employees to satisfy their own biological, social, and egoistic needs. They viewed their self-actualization as linked to pursuing company objectives.[126] The business of the company had become their own.

The development and pursuit of goals by employees provides significant opportunities for them to satisfy all sorts of human needs. This does not mean, however, that there will be no disagreements regarding the best ends and the means to those ends. What it does mean is that managers and employees can work together in the pursuit of mutual goals. Managers can discover previously hidden talents and creativity in their human resources unavailable in the absence of the goal-setting process.

While employee goal setting does not eliminate conflict and disagreement, it does provide a constructive tool for finding solutions to problems that integrate the objectives of the informal organization with those of the company. Goal setting can develop and nurture employee support, trust, and loyalty without significantly undermining managerial prerogatives. Goal setting is not a manipulative process for deluding employees into thinking they have been involved in managerial decisions. Employees will always know the difference between the decisions of management and their own. Any effort to deceive them can only be expected to increase distrust, hostility, and opposition.

The goal-setting process is not aimed at making employees feel important. Its purpose is to recognize their importance to the success of the company. The recognition itself is a significant motivational tool. Goal setting has nothing to do with manipulation or deception, and the process itself will be less effective if there is any hint of that taking place.

Managerial concerns regarding how they can meet employee goals stem from a misunderstanding of the process. Employee

126   Ibid., 175-176.

goals cannot be met by management. Managers will assist employees in working toward their own goals. Managers are ill equipped to cope with the emotional and status issues of the informal organization. The employees themselves must work to meet the goals they develop, redefine them as situations change, or abandon them when the goals no longer serve the employees' objectives. Management's role is one of facilitation and assistance.

The integration of the objectives of management with those of the informal organization is accomplished by allowing employees to take responsibility for their own desires and attitudes. The collective attitude of the informal organization becomes more positive as employees restate their negative, emotionally-charged criticisms of the workplace as desirable goals they hope to attain. The goal identification process develops ownership and hope.

7.

CREATING A SHARED VISION

When employees identify the issues that are relevant to them and develop goals to resolve those issues, morale improves very rapidly, and management can expect increased support by the informal organization as a whole. The next step in maintaining the ongoing support of the informal organization is to facilitate employee efforts to attain their goals. The involvement of management, however, is complicated by two troublesome characteristics of typical employee goals.

The first characteristic is that they are often vague and difficult to define. For example, a goal such as *Employees will enjoy their work* may seem impossible to define in an objective way. How can enjoyment be measured and quantified? Informal organizational goals tend to be emotionally based and can be defined only by the employees who formulate them. In the absence of clearly defined goals, it is impossible to determine whether and when those goals have been met, but maintaining the good will of the informal organization requires this. Therefore, a reliable method for leading employees in defining their goals is the topic of this chapter.

The second characteristic of most employee goals is that they may appear impossible to achieve due to costs, diversity of employee populations, the legal context of the goals, and other realities of the company. For example, a goal such as *Employees will be paid what they are worth* is impossible to define objectively, and depending on employee expectations, could involve costs that would be prohibitive to the company. Nevertheless, managers have nothing to fear. This difficulty is addressed by allowing the informal organization itself to own and attain the goals they have identified as relevant. In this way, management will not be blamed by employees for failures to meet goals developed and owned by the employees.

Before proceeding, it would be worthwhile to review a few of the reasons why it is necessary for management to put forth significant effort to engage the informal organization. Prolonged negativity and stagnation have the power to deprive a group of its vital creative energy. This often occurs after a string of negative events, managerial errors, and terminations of employment. Monotony can also decrease an organization's vital energy and contribute to an organizational climate dominated by a shared sense of hopelessness.

Employees working in a negative climate reinforce and perpetuate the situation through destructive communication. Open demonstrations of apathy, hostility, and scorn become the norm for the group, and all employees within the group are pressured to reinforce pessimistic perceptions. Attempts to introduce any optimistic views are resisted by the informal leadership as naïve.

In such an environment, informal organizations have no goals per se because employees are not in a position to develop them in the absence of managerial leadership. They see little or no use in working toward goals provided by management because the question "What's in it for me?" has not been answered. Their primary goal becomes obtaining the most compensation for the least amount of effort, and their secondary goals are aimed at meeting their needs for acceptance, status, and power.

The malaise of the informal organization can be significantly combated through the development of employee goals. This by itself, however, is not a long-term answer to the problem. Where goals are developed and forgotten, anger, hostility, and hopelessness are sure to return. Any long-term solution requires that employees be given opportunities to work toward their own goals while pursuing company objectives. When these opportunities are provided, pursuing company interests becomes the best way to realize employee goals.

The goals of the informal organization must ultimately be defined by its members. Managers facilitate this by engaging the group in developing its own vision for the future. Positive visions revitalize employees and provide them with a sense of purpose as well as opportunities to meet their self-actualizing needs. In developing these visions, employees define their goals in observable, objective terms that create excitement and support for company success.

Managers who lead employees through this process are often surprised at the visions employees provide for the goals they have developed. Goals such as *We will enjoy coming to work* take on specific meanings and, for that reason, become attainable. The fact that managers cannot understand employee goals in the absence of their assistance goes far to explain why attempts to merely appease informal organizations are typically fruitless. Only the employees themselves can define their goals and work to meet them. Managers who attempt to take this process from their employees bite off much more than they can chew.

Even among the employees who directly participate in the goal identification process, the precise meaning of their statements is not clear. Each employee has a slightly different idea of the meaning of each goal statement. Simply asking them to define their goals more precisely will not result in clearer thinking. This direct approach invites employees to spend much time arguing over the choice and meaning of words without ever getting to the underlying issues that are important to them. Employees need the time and opportunity to process their thoughts, desires, and expectations.

The vision development process increases enthusiasm and hope among employees by engaging their imagination. It offers opportunities for employees to meet their higher-order needs while they're at work as opposed to when they're away from it. Employees who develop visions from goals feel that they own their goals because they developed the visions that define them.

> **Managers can facilitate their employees in developing a positive vision of the company by doing the following on a regular basis:**
> 1. Review the goals.
> 2. Envision the ideal.
> 3. Share the vision.

1) Review the Goals

The process of vision development begins by reviewing the goals developed by employees to address the issues that are important to them. These are the objectives of the informal organization. The review itself goes far in assuring employees that management takes them seriously and that their input is important. Most employees have had the experience of identifying concerns only to have management ignore them.

Reviewing the goals emphasizes that management is listening and interested in employee concerns and ideas. Participants are acknowledged for their work in bringing their issues into the open and identifying ways to address them. Goals developed by a workgroup belong to the members of that group and are by definition relevant and important to them.

The acknowledgment of these goals by management sets the stage for an employee-management partnership that can revolutionize the extent of cooperation within the company. When the manager reviews the goals, a powerful message is sent that everyone is on the same page. For this reason, the manager should read the goals aloud to the group and acknowledge the hard work that went into the development of those goals. In this way, the employees' needs for recognition and respect are met as well.

In addition, the review of the goals is a preliminary and necessary step in developing a vision for the informal organization. Following the review, employees will be asked to create a vision for each goal reviewed. This amounts to determining the observable effects of meeting the goals. This sounds simple, but there are certain ways to accomplish it successfully, and it is an indispensible step in defining employee goals.

It is important to bear in mind that the employees identify the issues and problems they perceive in their workplace during the listening activity. They then state those problems positively as goals they would like to pursue. In this next activity, they will define their goals in objective terms that will facilitate meeting those goals and provide a means of determining whether they have been met.

2) Envision the Ideal

At this stage, management asks the employees to imagine what they would see once their goals have been met. Employees should identify as many observable outcomes for their goals as possible. For a goal such as *Employees will enjoy their work*, they should imagine what they would see if employees really did enjoy their roles in the company. They should be encouraged to brainstorm as many visions as possible.

For example, observable signs of employees enjoying their work would be arriving on time, missing fewer days due to illness, having potluck lunches occasionally in the lunchroom, and helping one another with difficult tasks. These observable behaviors become the vision of the goal as ideally attained.

Each goal should be addressed by identifying at least one but preferably many observable indicators that the goal has been reached. Though a single vision is acceptable, more visions are preferable because they provide more indicators of success, more opportunities to work toward the goal, and more chances for success. Eventually, employees will volunteer to bring about each of the visions they identify, and through their work for the group, they will increase their status and gain the respect of their peers.

The goals should be numbered, and the visions identified for each goal should be listed under them in a sort of outline for convenience. When the goals and their visions are listed in this way, they become a sort of blueprint for the informal organization and can be worked on as time permits during the regular course of business. As difficulties are encountered by the group in implementing the company's strategic plan, those can be addressed by translating them into goals, defining them as visions, and adding them to the list. This offers a release for employees and secures their continued cooperation in the implementation of the company's long-range plans.

An example of this is as follows:

I. MORALE (*Classification*)
  A. Employees will enjoy their work. (*Goal*)
   i. We will see employees arriving on time (*Vision*)
   ii. We will see employees missing fewer days due to illness (*Vision*)
   iii. We will see employees sharing potluck lunches (*Vision*)
   iv. We will see employees helping each other (*Vision*)
  B. (*Goal*)
   i. (*Vision*)
   ii. (*Vision*)

II. Overtime (*Classification*)
  A. Overtime will be assigned fairly. (*Goal*)
   i. (*Vision*)
   ii. (*Vision*)

It is important that employees understand that they are being asked to identify what they would *see* if the goal is met *ideally* as opposed to merely being met adequately. The manager should invite employees to imagine what the environment would be like in their workplace if their goals were met to the highest satisfaction of all employees. Envisioning the ideal excites employees and releases their energy and creativity in integrating their objectives with those of the company. There is no such thing as an unreasonable vision. Imagination is more important than facts at this point. Ambitious visions invite employees to reach their highest potential for the benefit of the company, and, in doing so, to tap into their talents and energy, which possibly have been withheld prior to this time.

If employees are properly encouraged to imagine the ideal work environment, their creativity will be engaged and they will experience a new sense of excitement about their goals. This excitement will provide new energy that can be channeled into the pursuit of both employee and management objectives. In addition, employee creativity will actually produce relevant and positive changes that will positively impact the morale of both managers and employees.

Employees typically ask if they shouldn't at least try to keep their visions realistic, and an inexperienced, overly cautious manager might be tempted to agree that they should. Unfortunately, this produces at least three undesirable results. The first is that the participants spend a great deal of time arguing over how realistic a given person's vision is.

The second is that the participants become angry with one another and disillusioned with the entire activity. Employees are embarrassed if the vision of a better tomorrow is condemned by coworkers as naïve. When employees worry about being laughed at or considered naïve, they are not free to participate, and the activity's usefulness can be dramatically impaired. Their status among their peers is threatened. Once this occurs, the entire activity is doomed to a negative spiral that will ultimately end in silence and hostility.

The third is that managers unwittingly offer their assistance in determining which visions are realistic and which are not. This results in employees feeling manipulated by an attempt to create the appearance that management's objectives are developed by the employees. Managers are once again placed in the position of saying no as an authority figure. Managers are not really in a position to speak to the issue of what is and what is not realistic because policymaking is a group activity. Company policy and the inevitable exceptions are ultimately determined by a group of managers acting together rather than one manager acting alone.

Instead, the better course is to request that ideal visions be developed. Employees are asked to imagine what they would see if their goals were ideally met. Imagination is much more important than knowledge in the success of this process. Asking for the ideal frees employees to be creative and managers to be supportive. Developing visions of the ideal workplace generates enthusiasm and hope. Rather than perpetuating the myth that managers are limiters and controllers, the process places managers in a supportive role as resources and facilitators.

The excitement generated by this process is essential to energizing the informal organization in the support of company objectives. Employees turn their attention from criticizing one another as being unrealistic and naïve to praising one another for their creative and positive visions. This lays the groundwork for employees to be encouraged by their peers in their support of company objectives and their cooperation with management. Management's concerns about the difficulties inherent in attempting to satisfy employee expectations arising from unrealistic visions are not warranted.

After all, if the vision is unrealistic given company resources, wouldn't the goal be impossible to meet? Couldn't this lead to employee unrest and even greater scorn for management? The answer to these questions is simply no. In the first place, management will not be charged with meeting any of the goals developed during this process because they are employee goals. The visions deal with goals that employees develop, define, and claim as their own—goals that will be addressed by employees through their informal organization. If the goals cannot be met, the employees will bear the failure or redefine them. They will not view this process as a failure of management because management has assisted them in pursuing these goals to the greatest extent possible from the outset.

The visions developed by the employees will be attainable even if they appear to be unrealistically ambitious because they will most likely deal with non-economic issues. In addition, the cooperation and support of the informal organization is capable of producing results that are nothing short of miraculous. The truth is that neither the employees nor management can know what is possible without developing a vision and attempting to make it reality. Most companies have never experienced the power that is unleashed when employees are fully cooperative.

In addition, the informal organization reacts just as most of us react when we have an unrealistic desire. We tend to redefine our unrealistic goals to make them attainable, or we abandon them. We modify our desires to coincide with reality and thereby make ourselves successful. The employees who comprise the informal organization deal with their desires in the same way. By authentically pursuing their positive visions, employees fulfill their needs for self-actualization, their efficiency increases, and they promote the interests of company, all at the same time.

3) Share the Vision

The process of envisioning what employees will observe when goals are met ideally, not just adequately, provides an energizing experience and a means for identifying whether those goals have been realized. Writing each vision statement with the words "I see" reinforces the idea that future improvements need to be observable and therefore attainable. Employees and the organization as a whole can be held accountable for conditions that are observable. Defining abstract concepts such as *Employees will enjoy working here* in terms of observable behaviors or conditions defines them and takes the power away from vague grumbling. If the vision is attained and employees feel that conditions have not improved, management can ask them to provide additional visions.

Vision development by employees should not be expected to remove all doubt and skepticism regarding the sincerity of management. However, it will open the door to positive efforts to improve group functioning and release the possibility for constructive interpretation of successes in realizing the group's visions. Participants leave the activity with excitement and commitment to the future that the skillful manager can direct. Instead of seeing the world through an opaque barrier they are free to be optimistic as they interpret managerial actions in a favorable light, or at least give management the benefit of the doubt until events can be discussed constructively. Employees are free to support the company continuously while processing difficulties and conflict as they arise without any decrease in effort.

The visions identified will be enthusiastically accepted and supported by all employees if they are accepted by the informal organization. Negative employees will be pressured by the others to get on board or face isolation. People are naturally drawn toward building a better future, and they need to be a member of a successful group. When a positive vision of the workplace is shared by the company and the informal organization, it becomes a powerful justification for any temporary uncertainty or sacrifices that may be required of the employees until their visions can be implemented. Negative employees will become supportive of company objectives even in the face of hardship to maintain their status among their peers.

When vision development is completed by a committee rather than the entire workgroup to make the number of participants manageable, it is critical that the visions identified for each goal be shared with the entire group to spread the enthusiasm of the participating committee and to integrate employee objectives with company objectives. When the high-status employees on the committee share those visions with the entire workgroup, their coworkers and supporters are bound to support them as well. High-status employees can thus use their influence on their peers to promote the interests of the company.

Failing to support the goals developed during this process is tantamount to refusing to support the employees who developed them. Those who would not support them soon find themselves confronted by the informal organization: their coworkers will exert peer pressure to gain their support. Those who do not wish to support the company will change their minds, lose the respect of their peers, or leave the company. Peer pressure within the workgroup is a powerful motivator.

The success of the company becomes an indispensible element in the pursuit of employees' goals and their visions of them. For example, if employees envision earning more for their work, they may learn while pursuing this goal how their efficiency affects their rates of pay. This may lead to an effort to increase company revenues through increased employee efficiency to make their vision a reality. Employees come to see that the success of the company is indispensible to the realization of their vision. This frees employees to be creative and self-motivated in the pursuit of what are now joint objectives. Managers are viewed as partners and facilitators in the pursuit of integrated objectives rather than as overseers and authority figures.

4) The Historical Foundation of Shared Visions

In the 1930s, Elton Mayo noted that one of the primary contributors to conflict in the workplace was that employees lacked a community of interest in the work of the company. Workers did not perceive a relationship between their work and the quality of their lives other than their need for compensation. Their work was simply something they needed to do in order to do what they wanted to do during the rest of their lives outside of work. The interests of employees were not integrated with those of the company.

There was no significant evidence that the abstract nature of their work was responsible for poor employee attitudes and motivation. Observations of managers provided no evidence that defective supervision was an important contributing factor. Nevertheless, there seemed to be conflicting opinions that ultimately produced discord regarding the nature of the work and how it was performed.[127] This resulted in management and employees working at cross purposes much of the time, and the conflict could not be understood or controlled. Employees simply did not accept management's vision of the company.

Careful planning is not enough to ensure the smooth operation of any company. The emotionally detached, logic-based administration of management's strategic plans is not enough to generate employee support. Employees are almost universally hostile to directives communicated on a take-it-or-leave-it basis regardless of how advantageous or logical the orders may appear to managers. While managers view their directives as necessary to increase efficiency and profits for the company, employees view them as personally irrelevant. For the employees, working provides a living and an opportunity to meet their needs for status and acceptance by their peers.

Mayo noted that it is difficult for employees to perform work consistently and with excellence in the absence of seeing its purpose.[128] It doesn't matter how motivated they may be initially; employees have difficulty persisting in working without some vision of an objective that relates to them personally. This effect

---

127   Mayo, *The Human Problems of an Industrial Civilization*, 119.
128   Ibid., 120.

is exacerbated by the size and complexity of the formal organizations of the companies for which they work. In the absence of a vision to orient employees to the importance of their work, they feel that they have little or no responsibility for its quality.

In the 1940s, Chester Barnard noted that the opportunity for participation in company decisions and problem solving is very highly valued by employees.[129] Employees have a need to be involved in the inner workings of the company. This need is sometimes related to status and prestige. Participation in the process of developing a vision for the workplace meets these and other self-actualizing needs. The process itself motivates and energizes employees by providing them an opportunity to integrate their personal interests with those of the company to the point that the successes of the workgroup are viewed as their personal successes.

Employees who participate in developing visions recognize the importance of their contributions and the importance of cooperation and teamwork within the company as a whole. It is natural for employees to prefer to work with large, socially important, and economically successful organizations. Visioning provides an opportunity for comradeship among the participants. It encourages a climate of mutual support and the development of positive personal attitudes. The informal organization is based on communication among its members.[130] Positive communication among employees is essential to the operation of every company because the content of that communication affects employee perceptions.

Negative communication among employees within the informal organization can be the basis of hostility and the development of employee norms that are inconsistent with the success of the company. At any given time, both negative and positive communications are taking place among employees. This is a reality that

---

129   Barnard, *The Functions of the Executive*, 147-148.
130   Ibid., 148-149.

visioning goes far to manage. Negative attitudes are inevitable to some extent because the desires of employees are unstable and reflect the instability of their lives. Incentives that are supported by informal organizations of employees positively impact employee behavior while those that are scorned are ineffective.

Since employee cooperation cannot be maintained over the long term by coercion or incentives, management of the informal organization is essential. Coercion leads to employee hostility and sabotage while incentives are never universally appealing among employees. To avoid these shortcomings, Chester Barnard advocated the rationalization of incentives in the early 1960s. He and other leading managers came to view this as a method of persuasion far superior to the use of either coercion or incentives.[131]

Visioning is an excellent and effective way to enlist the support of the informal organization; this is accomplished through the rationalization of incentives, which amounts to convincing employees that it is in their best interest to do a certain thing. Much effort is expended in our society to rationalize the desires of consumers through salesmanship, advertising, and outright propaganda concerning the desirability of various products. Unfortunately, the same effort has not been expended to rationalize the desires of employees. Most companies are ineffective at convincing their employees that when they pursue company objectives through their work, they are actually pursuing their own best interests.

The development of employee visions allows management to identify incentives that actually appeal to employees. Not only do the visions identified by employees have a natural appeal, but their power is maintained by peer pressure among the employees through their informal organizations. Even the best incentives developed by managers in the absence of this process lose effectiveness eventually due to the changeability of employee desires. Because incentives offered by management are typically economic in nature, they fail to meet employees' self-actualizing needs.

---

131   Ibid., 150-151.

When employee needs for compensation are met, the power of economic incentives decreases and the desire for self-actualizing incentives increases.

The needs for status, acceptance, and respect are powerful, and for the most part, they are met by the employees themselves within their informal organization. Defining goals in terms of visions rationalizes these incentives and engages the informal organization in motivating employees to pursue company objectives. Employees earn acceptance, status, and respect by successfully performing their work and meeting company goals. It is well established that people will not work for anything they are not convinced benefits them in some way. Employees must be convinced that their work will benefit them beyond their wages. Developing and pursuing their own visions captures otherwise wasted effort and helps employees identify the success of their company with their own interests.

Non-material incentives often conflict with each other. The opportunity for one employee to gain personal prestige as an incentive often involves the loss of prestige for another employee. Balancing this effect among employees is an impossible task for management, but it is entirely possible for the informal organization to accomplish. In fact, that is precisely the business of informal organizations of employees. The informal organization has the power to rationalize and balance non-material incentives by creating niches that allow employees to gain some sense of status within the organization. The key to engaging the informal organization is to provide an opportunity for employees to work together on mutually held goals and visions perceived as important by their workgroup.

Managers who engage their employees in this way benefit personally as well. Interestingly, employees view the managers who lead them through this process as visionary, charismatic, and inspirational. Leading employees through the process of developing visions, making changes to fit their visions, and encouraging them to reach their long-term goals allows the manager to practice transformational leadership. Researchers have found that transformational leadership is associated with superior performance within business units.[132]

Transformational leaders develop clear visions and strategies for attaining them. They are confident and optimistic as they encourage employees to work toward their visions. They demonstrate confidence in their subordinates and celebrate small steps to build their confidence as they work toward making their visions reality.[133] In fact, a significant body of research indicates that transformational leadership is more effective than other forms. It is effective both in the United States and abroad, and it is preferred by employees the world over.[134] Developing visions and working toward them provides employees with a sense of purpose that inspires them in whatever work they undertake.

At least one study suggests that high-performing leaders are more visionary than their less successful colleagues. In that study, 72 percent of high-performing leaders were described as visionary compared to only 34 percent of the less successful leaders.[135] While this type of study does not demonstrate causation, it does suggest that managers who lead their employees by developing visions are positively perceived by their employees. Managers who enjoy the respect and support of their employees experience less stress and make fewer mistakes than those who are at odds with the people they supervise.

The documentation of this activity can create a plan for the future in outline form. Once all employee goals have been classified and listed with visions of what will be seen when they have been accomplished, the manager has a powerful tool that can be used to continuously engage employees in integrating their

---

132   J. M. Howell and B. J. Avolio, "Transformational leadership, transactional leadership, locus of control, and support of innovation: Key predictors of consolidated-business-unit performance," *Journal of Applied Psychology* 78, no. 6 (1993): 891-902.

133   G. A. Yukl, *Leadership in Organizations*, 3rd ed. (Englewood Cliffs, NJ: Prentice Hall, 1994).

134   B. M. Bass, "Does the transactional-transformational leadership paradigm transcend organizational and national boundaries?" *American Psychologist* 52, no. 2 (1997): 130-139.

135   J. W. Hunt and B. Laing, "Leadership: The role of the exemplar," *Business Strategy Review* 8, no. 1 (1997): 31-42.

interests with those of the company. The pursuit of this plan by employees will maintain the alignment of employee desires with the objectives of management. Furthermore, creating action steps allows communication to become continuous between employees and management. This improved, continuous communication will maintain the alignment achieved through listening, goal setting, and vision development.

A shared vision defines what is desirable for employees and eliminates much of the inconsistency and conflict that often occurs among employees and between employees and managers. Employees' visions of a better workplace cannot be ignored or devalued. When developed as suggested in this chapter, these visions will provide new energy in the workplace and will foster an understanding of the interdependence of employees and management—the informal organization and the company.

8.

INTEGRATING ORGANIZATIONAL OBJECTIVES

When employees create visions of their optimal workplace, questions naturally arise regarding just how those visions can become reality. Vision statements are restatements of the participants' hopes for a better future that entail more opportunities and greater benefits. Typical questions relate to the appropriate procedures for implementing employee goals; others concern who should shoulder the responsibility for taking the required steps. Finding the answers to these questions is an ongoing task that will maintain the support of their informal organization indefinitely. The manager's role will be to facilitate this inquiry and provide information and advice. When goals cannot be met, employees will understand why, and they will either abandon those goals or redefine them.

The process of finding answers to these questions and others engages employees and fully integrates the objectives of the informal organization with those of the company. The work necessary to realize employee visions will provide members of the group with opportunities to have their higher-order needs met as well as ongoing opportunities for positive interactions between members of the group and management. When visions are too vague or so infeasible as to be unattainable, management will not be blamed. Instead, employees will have a greater understanding of the business, economic, and legal environment in which their company operates.

It is natural for a manager to be concerned with questions regarding what to do if the group's goals cannot be met because they are too time consuming, unrealistic, inefficient, or costly.

Many managers fear that employee goals may conflict with managerial directives or the strategic plans of the organization. The specter of dealing with disappointment can be daunting. In practice, however, these problems are easily handled because they are owned by the employees. These are questions and problems for which the employees will find answers and solutions as they pursue their visions. Unrealistic goals will be modified or abandoned, but many seemingly unrealistic goals will be met to the satisfaction of employees and the astonishment of management. The work of employees to attain their visions of the ideal workplace fully integrates their goals with those of the company because the success of their efforts is dependent on the success of the company.

The final and ongoing step in the process of securing the support of employee informal organizations is the development of action steps by employees. This further defines the visions of the workgroup by requiring employees to reconcile their desires with the "law of the situation." The law of the situation is impersonal and governs managers and employees alike. What the situation requires of those who work for the company is much more readily accepted than any directive of management based on power and authority alone. If employees cannot attain a certain goal, the environment within which the company exists is responsible rather than management or the board of directors.

Determining what is necessary to make a vision for the future a reality in the present provides employees with ownership, responsibility, and opportunities to have their self-actualizing needs met by the process itself. It is critical that the employees themselves develop the action steps rather than the manager. This can be difficult because most managers develop action steps as a matter of course every time they give instructions or conclude a meeting in which a plan of action is developed. It is natural, therefore, for managers to want to jump in and do this for the employees. However, the steps must be developed by the employees, because they are the ones who will ultimately have the responsibility for implementing them, and for their success or failure. Actually taking the steps developed brings employees face to face with the business realities that managers encounter every day. Once this occurs, managers are no longer the scapegoats for environmental factors outside their control. The law of the situation is in control.

Any manager who attempts to develop action steps without employee involvement will acquire some responsibility for the implementation of those steps. Employees feel responsible for ideas that come from them. If the manager develops the action plans or participates to any greater degree than simply serving as a resource to the group, the action steps developed may be viewed by the employees as unrealistic burdens being imposed by management to further interests that are not consistent with their own. Action steps developed by management that don't work are evidence of management's incompetence or, worse, evidence of managerial sabotage. Having the employees create the action steps minimizes this danger.

Employees dislike being ordered about. In fact, one of the most frequent sources of discontent among employees is being directed to implement decisions without being asked for their ideas regarding how implementation can be accomplished. This not only annoys them, but it stifles their creativity and cooperation as well. It decreases their sense of responsibility for the outcomes. Allowing employees to develop their own action steps provides them with the ownership of those steps as well as the outcomes, and it strengthens the bond between them and the company. The action steps must consist entirely of the employees' ideals of how to attain their visions. Managers may assist when asked, but they should allow employees to develop their own steps.

When employees contribute to the formulation of action steps, they bring their expertise and creativity to the table and actively participate in making their visions become reality. Their beliefs and desires are incorporated into the mission of the organization through participation in this critical task. Employee visions can be attained only if the company is efficient and profitable. Managers who merely identify what they consider the obvious steps necessary to accomplish and direct employees accordingly do not understand that it is the employees' participation in developing or modifying the action steps that creates employee ownership.

New procedures are often viewed as annoying extra work by employees who have not participated in the planning process, but those who have participated look forward to implementing the procedures, and they view any difficulties that arise as interesting challenges that can make their jobs meaningful and exciting. Developing action steps increases the positive energy of employee workgroups by allowing them to take the natural step from planning to action.

> **Managers can facilitate the development of action steps by employees in the following way:**
>   1. **Revisit employee issues.**
>   2. **Identify action steps.**
>   3. **Integrate the vision.**

1) Revisit Employee Issues

By the time employees have defined their issues and problems as goals and further refined them as visions, much work has been accomplished within the informal organization. From this juncture, it is possible to discuss employee issues in an atmosphere characterized by goodwill and cooperation rather than the hostility that existed when management first implemented the listening process. More than ever before, employees are aware that the success of the company is critical to effecting the positive changes they desire.

Each time employees discuss their visions for the future, they are revisiting their issues in positive terms. Now, however, employees are no longer complaining about management and its unwillingness to meet their needs. They are discussing their own solutions to their problems and the best way to implement their solutions. Managers are viewed as partners in the pursuit of the common good.

Encouraging members of a workgroup to discuss their visions of how to improve their work environment improves morale and instills hope for a better future. Managers who show an interest in these visions are perceived as supportive and visionary. The perceived differences between the interests of management and employees diminish, thus opening the door for new levels of cooperation. Managers are viewed as team members with specialized roles rather than just authority figures.

When members of a group discuss their ideas for improvement, they reconsider their visions, but more specifically, they define them. Discussions encourage the participants to agree on what they desire and how they will know if their needs have been met. This fosters employee ownership of ideas and ensures the support of the informal organization in working toward a better future. In fact, it is primarily through discussion that the informal group realizes that its interests are intimately tied to management's.

Employee ownership of visions is a prerequisite to the integration of employee and company objectives. The ownership of visions brings responsibility for their realization and opportunities for distinction to employees that cannot be conferred otherwise. Management must be supportive of employee visions without taking responsibility for them. Managers may play the part of facilitators, cheerleaders, and advisors, but they need to avoid the temptation to take over.

The discussion and celebration of visions developed using this method recognizes employees for their creativity and professionalism. The discussions themselves help meet some of their needs for status, recognition, and respect from both management and peers. At the same time, the concept of the company as a unique entity takes on new meaning for the employees. Not only is it a source of income, but without its success, the visions the employees develop cannot be realized.

2) Identify Action Steps

After employees have had opportunities to review, explain, and celebrate their visions, it is time to take the final step in the process, which involves integrating their goals with those of the company. Keep in mind that visions are the observable evidence that the goals formulated by employees to address specific issues have been met. The action steps summarize the specific steps employees must take to make their visions reality. Action steps let employees know where to begin, and they provide a point of focus as employees make important contributions to their own satisfaction with the company. The process of developing a few necessary action steps for realizing visions establishes ownership for the visions within the informal organization. Employees rather than managers use their creativity and experience to determine just how to go about making something wonderful into a day-to-day reality for the workgroup.

To begin the process, the manager simply divides the workgroup or employee committee into subgroups of five or six employees. The visions are then divided among the subgroups as equally as possible to make the task manageable. Each subgroup is then asked to identify at least three steps necessary to make each vision a reality and thereby accomplish the stated goals.

Because this will require a great deal of discussion and brainstorming, the task may need to be completed over a period of weeks depending on the time available. During this period, managers may expect renewed cooperation and reduced tension within the workgroup. The identification of these steps reinforces management's sincere support for this process and redefines their roles as facilitators and consultants in assisting their employees as they work toward reaching their goals.

One of the first things managers new to this process observe is that it is much easier to state what needs to be done than it is to do it. In fact, it is impossible to identify every step necessary to make any vision become reality. Employees often express disagreement over which step should be taken first and how many steps a task might require. The solution to this problem is simply to ask employees to identify as many steps as they can, and inform them that the action steps they identify may be revised as necessary by the employees who volunteer to work on them. The purpose of formulating the steps for each vision is merely to provide ideas or starting points for those who are interested in working to improve the company.

A manager who might have been concerned that a goal could require increased expenditures will come to see that most employee goals will not cost the company much, if anything at all. Very modest expenditures or changes in policy or procedure go a long way toward maintaining the good will produced by this process. In situations in which the action steps require expenditures, employees should include a step in which they or their supervisor consults with the company officer in charge of the necessary funds. If funding is not available, the employees can brainstorm ways in which they can raise the funds needed. This often leads to ideas regarding cost savings and sharing the profits from increased efficiency. In this situation, employees are not being told that management won't meet their demands. Instead, they are learning why conditions are as they are, and they will cooperate with management to improve those conditions. The employees themselves come to appreciate the bottom line faced by managers.

Most of the time, employees will be able to carry out the action steps they identify to produce the changes they desire within the workplace. In instances where they cannot, they will not blame management. Instead, they will educate themselves regarding the obstacles they have encountered and then brainstorm ways to overcome them. They realize that they and their managers are subject to Mary Follett's "law of the situation." The situation rather than management is telling them no. Understanding this concept frees the employees to appeal to management and each other for help in circumventing the difficulties they have encountered. For example, when raises cannot be provided, employees are faced with the questions of whether they are facing an economic reality or an efficiency problem. Interestingly, they are likely more capable of improving efficiency than management can do alone because they actually do the day-to-day work that may need to be reorganized.

This places management and employees on the same team attacking a common problem—the situation. Neither management nor the employees may ignore the law of the situation. Situations lend themselves to interventions, and finger pointing is viewed as the waste of time it really is. But even when visions simply cannot be met, there are no scapegoats. Employees abandon them or redefine them as something that can be brought into existence. They do this because they own the visions and can change them to meet their needs. The process of developing visions, working toward them, achieving them, or redefining them is ongoing. It serves to maintain continued, cooperative communication between management and employees. This is a key feature of companies that have fully integrated the objectives of management and employees to maximize cooperation.

During the action step identification process, managers can provide data and advice to assist their employees. Doing so broadens employees' thinking, refines their attitudes, and encourages them to support company initiatives. It would be well to recall at this point that the issues, goals, and visions of the informal organization are often only tangential to those of management. The informal organization is primarily concerned with meeting the self-actualizing needs of employees. Consequently, its visions are usually consistent with the formal operations of the company. Apparent inconsistencies are typically superficial, and the development of action steps will dispel apparent inconsistencies in most instances. Employees cannot meet their self-actualizing needs if the company is not profitable. In fact, the more efficient a company is in its competitive environment, the more opportunities there are for employees to meet their self-actualizing needs.

Consider, for example, a situation in which employees envision more breaks during their workday. Developing action steps to accomplish this will inevitably lead to the changes that will make longer breaks possible. However, the employees' daily work still needs to be done. Would employees be willing to work longer to make the extended breaks possible? If not, other approaches to dealing with the problem underlying the desire for longer breaks can be suggested and explored. Employees with creative ideas will be rewarded with higher status within the informal organization. The entire pursuit is likely to benefit the company as well, because one way to provide more time is for employees to perform their work more efficiently.

If efficiencies can be identified to produce the additional break time desired, that can solve the problem. If they cannot, employees will likely abandon the idea as unworkable under the circumstances. The important point is that the situation dictates what is possible and what is not rather than an authoritarian manager or a militant workforce. There is no need to use power or intimidation to force the other side to concede to additional break time. There are no winners if the visions cannot be realized and no losers if they can. Managers and employees are on the same team.

Whereas management has been viewed as the obstacle in the past, it comes to be viewed as a supporter. Company objectives are consistent with those of the informal organization, and both the company and its informal employee organizations work toward them. If visions and objectives cannot be realized, they violate the impersonal law of the particular situation, and no one is to blame. Since employees and managers are allies working for the same outcomes, problems rather than people and personalities are the focus of attention. Instead of power being used to force one side or the other to concede to a demand, mutual creativity is applied to solve the problems of the company.

In his role-playing exercises for managers, Norman Maier cited examples of typical issues of concern to employees. The issues he identified included ways to alleviate boredom, ways to make work more interesting, ways to bring variety into the work day, and even ways to break up the work period to avoid fatigue.[136] Identifying specific action steps necessary for nebulous goals such as these would be next to impossible for the manager to develop without the assistance of those who set them. Attempts on the part of management alone to meet the employees' needs for interesting work are doomed from the outset. Complex problems such as these can be addressed only through a process that intimately involves employees in the definition and solution of those problems.

Once a workgroup has processed its desires enough to agree on its visions, questions arise regarding scheduling, trial runs, and the potential effects of proposals on specific employees. This is when the employees launch the problem-solving process. Excellent communication plays a key role in allowing the group's visions to evolve into specific outcomes without stagnating at the level of mere abstract statements of hopes for the future. The development of action steps facilitates communication and focuses the attention of employees on the realities of attaining their visions.

The group's solutions to the problems that arise must remain subject to change as part of an ongoing communication process. The needs of individuals within a group are constantly changing; because of this continual state of flux, the decisions aimed at satisfying those needs must evolve. When the informal organization is given the freedom to address its own issues within the context of

---

136   Maier, Solem, and Maier, *Supervisory & Executive Development*, 275.

the economic realities of the company, virtually all members of the group will find themselves a part of the decision-making process. Defensive behaviors and resistance to change will evaporate.[137]

3) Integrate the Vision

After the workgroup has grappled with the question of how to make their visions reality by identifying action steps, the combined visions of the participants can be integrated into a single, comprehensive plan for the company. This integration can be embodied in a document listing categories of employee concerns, goals that address them, visions of ideal solutions to employee concerns, and suggestions for the initial steps necessary to improve the situation. The plan provides an outline for the maintenance of efficiency and cooperation through an ongoing dialogue between management and employees.

An example of such a document is as follows:

I. MORALE (*Concern Classification*)
  A. Employees will enjoy their work (*Goal*)
   i. We will arrive on time (*Vision*)
        1. Employees will be informed of this goal
        2. Employees will car pool
   ii. We will miss fewer days due to illness (*Vision*)
        1. Employees will call in ill at least eight hours before their shift.
        2. Employees ill more than three days per month will provide documentation from a doctor.
   iii. We will share potluck lunches (*Vision*)
        1. The date will be cleared with management
        2. Arrangements will be made to store food
        3. Employees will be asked to bring something
        4. Volunteers will be found for serving and clean up.

---

137   Ibid., 191-192.

    iv. We will help each other (Vision)
- 1. (*Action Step*)
- 2. (*Action Step*)
- 3. (*Action Step*)

  B. (*Goal*)
    i. (*Vision*)
- 1. (*Action Step*)
- 2. (*Action Stop*)

    ii. (*Vision*)
- 1. (*Action Step*)
- 2. (*Action Step*)

II. Overtime (*Concern Classification*)

  A. Overtime will be fairly assigned. (*Goal*)
    i. All employees have equal opportunities to work overtime (*Vision*)
- 1. (*Action Step*)
- 2. (*Action Step*)

    ii. Employees will earn more than they currently earn. (*Vision*)
- 1. (*Action Step*)
- 2. (*Action Step*)
- 3. (*Action Step*)

    iii. Overtime will not be required during holidays (*Vision*)
- 1. (*Action Step*)
- 2. (*Action Step*)

  B. (*Goal*)
    i. (*Vision*)
- 1. (*Action Step*)
- 2. (*Action Step*)

    ii. (Vision)
- 1. (*Action Step*)
- 2. (*Action Step*)

III. Opportunities for Advancement (*Concern Classification*)

A. (*Goal*)

  i. (*Vision*)

      1. (*Action Step*)

      2. (*Action Step*)

      3. (*Action Step*)

  ii. (*Vision*)

      1. (*Action Step*)

      2. (*Action Step*)

This outline is the physical embodiment of the integrated objectives of the informal organization of employees and the company. It is a blueprint for ongoing dialogue that will maintain open communication and a means for integrating company and employee objectives as conflicts arise. As employees review and discuss this outline among themselves, the process of integration is in full sway. The approval and support of management plays a critical role in ensuring the continued support of employees. The directives of management that do not directly concern the visions of employees, and thus are not listed in the outline, are viewed as necessary preconditions to improving the situation for employees. Conflicts are opportunities for creative cooperation and mutual support within the company. They are resolved by the law of the situation rather than by force or intimidation.

Once this outline has been completed, it should be distributed to all employees. If a committee was utilized instead of the entire workgroup due to its size, the employees who developed it should be the ones to share it with their peers. Managers are cheerleaders and facilitators in this process rather than leaders. The vision for a better future was developed by employees and therefore belongs to them. Allowing the high-status employees who developed the outline to present it helps to meet their needs for recognition and increases their ownership of it.

Ultimately, the combined vision will be adopted by the entire workgroup, or it will be revisited by them simply because it is the articulated vision of the informal organization. Employees will support it or at least face peer pressure to do so. Any preliminary concerns should be handled by welcoming discussion and reminding everyone that the employees themselves may edit the plans at any time. The process itself affects the values of the group. However, if changes and adjustments are warranted, they can be made with ease.

Even those who do not support the plan are drawn into participating in its revision. This creates numerous opportunities for leadership, education, and integration of company and employee interests. Employees who chronically oppose management find themselves drawn in by the excitement of the process itself. The informal organization has a great deal of power to dictate how events are interpreted and the relative value of incentives.

4) The Historical Foundation of Action Step Development

In the 1950s, Norman Maier consistently advocated group approaches to problem solving. When the suggestions and visions of the entire workgroup are considered, no one feels accused or devalued. Problems are placed before the entire group in a constructive way that involves them in finding joint, workable solutions. Peer pressure for cooperation with management becomes a motivating force that encourages employees to work toward meeting company objectives without placing management in the role of the enforcer.[138]

When members of an informal organization have worked to identify the steps necessary to make their visions reality, they have further refined what they meant or have even redefined their desires. Any mistakes they have made will simply be corrected by their peers in further discussions of the action steps once

---

138. Ibid., 109-110.

implementation begins. When the vision has been presented and discussed among employees, implementation becomes part of an ongoing communication process between management and employees that maintains the integration of employee and company interests. Special meetings do not need to be called unless employees request them and the process will not be time consuming. Managers simply add an item regarding implementation of employee visions to the agendas of their regular meetings.

The process of working on action steps and the interactions that arise from this work are at least as important as the visions themselves in meeting the higher-order needs of employees. For example, if a disgruntled group of employees lists improving morale as a goal and envisions that all employees will enjoy their work, managers may not know exactly what to do. Exactly how does one go about making work enjoyable for another? By asking employees to develop action steps that will help make this vision reality, the problem is delivered to the employees themselves. Rather than take a defensive posture, management shows concern and assures employees that they want to improve the situation. Instead of attempting to determine what exactly is meant by enjoying one's work, management simply asks the employees themselves what can be done to improve the situation.

Any attempt by management to address such an emotionally based issue as this would be doomed at the outset. Only the employees themselves have the power to address how they feel about their work. By asking the employees to identify the steps necessary to help employees enjoy their work, management successfully engages employee creativity and creates opportunities for leadership within their informal organization.

The action step identified by employees may be as simple as having a potluck luncheon so that employees can get to know one another better. Management can support this idea by allowing the employees who show a special interest in the idea to plan and organize it. If during a discussion following the luncheon employees express the belief that their vision of employees enjoying their work has been realized, managers may assume that morale has been improved. Morale is a concern of both employees and management.

There are several important features of this example to consider, the first of which is that without the involvement of the workgroup itself, management would have had no practical idea of what the employees meant when they expressed their vision as a need to enjoy their work. Ignoring a situation in which employees don't like their work or attempting to unilaterally improve morale is neither wise nor practical. In the absence of the processes discussed here, simply attempting to locate and question a few disgruntled employees would only create suspicion and reinforce the idea that management is somehow responsible for the discontent. By asking the group what to do through the action step identification process, the employees who did not enjoy their work are involved in a setting in which they can become the leaders.

It is important to note that in the foregoing example, the potluck luncheon was not the active force in improving employee morale. That was accomplished by suggesting a luncheon, having it approved, organizing it, and executing it. The employees who became involved were able to gain status within the informal organization through their participation. Since the luncheon took place at work, the company became an important source of an activity designed to meet the employees' self-actualizing needs. This alone makes employees more supportive. After all, without the company, these opportunities to meet higher order needs through increasing status and providing leadership would not exist.

Generally, the necessary process to achieve goals developed in this manner will not involve company policies or require a significant expenditure of resources. In the example of the potluck luncheon, the employees organized the luncheon themselves at little cost to the company. This or something like it is the rule rather than the exception. If managers had been insightful enough to have guessed that a luncheon was desired and thus had attempted to organize it themselves, it is fairly certain that they would not have met with such success. Employees are meeting self-actualizing *emotional* needs rather than economic needs when they plan and enact an event such as this for themselves. Their economic needs were more or less already met adequately in the form of regular pay. In fact, emotional needs rarely take priority until employees' needs for security and economic stability are met.

In the relatively rare instance in which the fulfillment of employee visions will involve the expenditure of scarce company resources or increased compensation, the action steps developed by employees will entail visits with company executives who are responsible for controlling the budgets that will be affected. These visits will educate them regarding the economic realities of the company without creating the "us versus them" mentality that is so often seen in union negotiations. When employees are taken seriously and allowed to gather data, they will more readily accept the facts they find and revise their desires accordingly in an effort to be reasonable. The participation in this process by employees maintains their good will even when their visions cannot be realized due to the costs involved.

In instances such as these, management plays the role of educator. By answering the questions raised by employees attempting to realize a costly vision, management effectively makes the situation the obstacle to be overcome (if that is feasible). Management is not placed in the position of a powerful other that will deny employee requests unless overpowered. Instead, it is viewed as supporting the ideas of the employees and working with them to obtain the necessary funding. If productivity can be increased or costs reduced, management can offer increased compensation. Otherwise, compensation will need to remain unchanged until the situation improves. Both management and employees are subject to the law of the situation.

Employees faced with data that show that their request is unworkable inform each other much more efficiently and with much greater legitimacy than management ever could. When employees have investigated and learned the underlying facts of the situation, they are much more believable conduits for this information than managers are. They have more credibility among their fellow employees, and managers are removed from the role of negative authority figures that do nothing but frustrate employee initiatives. Managers are viewed as supportive of employee ideas, but similarly, they are bound by the facts.

If no other source of funding can be found, employees typically revise their action steps or abandon the vision altogether. However, in cases in which they abandon their unworkable vision, the effect on morale is much different than it is when management simply says no to their request. Visions abandoned by the informal organization are scrapped because they are unworkable in the situation in which the employees find themselves rather than because management doesn't care or has scorn for employee desires. Most employees will find the former acceptable while the latter invites them to increase their power within the company and withhold cooperation.

In the 1950s, Maier advocated the creation of a free and permissive atmosphere for communication regarding problems affecting the workgroup. Managers should understand that even in situations involving poor performance, the problem is not inefficiency or inadequate production. These are only symptoms of the real problems. Once the problems experienced by the workgroup have been identified and addressed, other problems are either much easier to address or simply vanish of their own accord. In other words, working toward employee goals can be expected to solve apparently unrelated problems within the company.

When a manager invites discussion of difficulties and acknowledges their validity, the discussion will turn to ways for improving the job.[139] This greatly reduces blaming and turns the energy and creativity of employees toward solving their own problems as well as increasing efficiency and productivity. This approach builds morale and trust. The problem-solving that results from identifying action steps encourages new thinking and inventive ways to address the mutual concerns of the employees and the company. Employees learn to evaluate proposed solutions on their merits, which helps them to support the economically based objectives of management. Managers engaging in this process must be consistently permissive in communication and sensitive to the concerns and feelings of employees. Fostering full participation in the process increases its effectiveness and lays the groundwork for the continuing support of all employees within the company.

In the 1940s, Chester Barnard noted that a key purpose of executive functions should be to maintain cooperative effort within their organizations or departments.[140] Merely managing a group of people is not enough. The essential functions of managers are to foster communication, secure the effort of employees, and define purpose. This can be done only with the participation of the employees themselves and not for them. Listening is the central element in fostering communication between employees and managers. Managers who listen and are not intimidated by what they hear have gone far to perform this essential executive function. The processes described in this and previous chapters merely provide the means for leading employees in constructive communication with one another and with management. As employees discuss the concerns of the informal system, they formulate joint purposes and integrate their objectives with those of the company.

The process of using employee concerns to develop a shared vision for the company helps develop the belief that employees and the company share a common purpose. The development of this essential belief explains much of the educational and

---

139   Maier, Solem, and Maier, *Supervisory & Executive Development*, 275.
140   Barnard, *The Functions of the Executive*, 216-217.

morale-building work in industrial organizations as well as strictly political and religious organizations.[141] What is suggested here is merely that this process is the basis of a cooperative relationship. The chapters that follow will discuss ways in which management can maintain the good will and support of the informal organization once it has been secured. When an atmosphere is created in which employees are free to communicate with management, new levels of cooperation are possible. Employee creativity and even volunteerism become available in ways they were not previously.

The key to managing the informal organization lies in having a genuine concern for employees. No company can be successful in the absence of the individual successes of its employees. The welfare of every company is inextricably entwined with the people it employs . When management and employees are brought to recognize their community of interest, both the company and its employees are free to reach their potential. In actuality, management cannot choose *not* to communicate with employees. When management fails to listen or attempts to silence employees, the amount of negative talk among employees will increase dramatically. They will speak to one another and foment discontent when managers refuse to listen. Cooperation will become strained or impossible when employees think in terms of "us versus them."

---

141   Ibid., 87.

9.

CAPITALIZING ON OPEN COMMUNICATION

Once the lines of communication have been opened and the interests of employees have been integrated with those of the company, employees are free to identify with the company itself. Continuous communication is necessary to maintain the support of the informal organization. Regular meetings with employees are useful to make assignments, check progress, and combat reversion to old practices. They also provide an acceptable forum for dealing with unanticipated consequences and negative outcomes while engaging the informal organization in problem solving. Conflict and unanticipated problems are inevitable. However, in companies with open communication, regular meetings with active listening become opportunities to improve rather than provide the reasons employees withhold their cooperation.

Employees in most companies communicate among themselves in the absence of the manager. Rumors and misinformation are often circulated within the informal employee organization, and attempts by management to set the record straight are viewed with suspicion. However, when managers open the communication process by leading their staff through the communication processes of listening, goal setting, visioning, and action step development fundamentally change the nature of the communication within their workgroups. Once employees have engaged in these processes, the manager becomes an accepted part of the employee communication network and can play a significant role in assuaging the kind of negative employee communication that damages morale.

After the initial processes have been completed, the employees and the manager will become more efficient in their communication. For example, when employees volunteer negative issues in conversations with the manager, they will also immediately suggest goals, visions, and action steps. Managers familiar with the process will listen and lead employees in brainstorming solutions without taking ownership of the problems. The open discussion of problems circumvents the underground rumor network, thus effectively stopping those problems from turning into conflicts. Instead, employees engage managers in the problem-solving process immediately. This reduces stress and increases cooperation and coordination within the workgroups in which this type of communication evolves. The communication processes evolve into a consistent group problem-solving process that maintains communication and supportive relationships. Frequent, open communication presents ideal opportunities to allow those who identify problems to present them, to identify solutions, and to meet their self-actualizing needs by making their visions reality.

When employees identify problems to managers in private, but they don't want to present them to the group, managers should present those concerns as though they were their own and ask for the assistance of the group in determining how to address them. Employees wishing to bring matters before their informal organization for reconsideration may be hesitant to do so if they believe their ideas may be unwelcome. They feel a need to have their issues considered, but they are hesitant to risk the disapproval of their peers. In their minds, either management or the informal employee organization is responsible for their discontent. When the manager volunteers to take their issues before the employee group for consideration, they feel they have found an ally in the manager, and they realize that management is not responsible for the problem situation. This allows disagreements to be discussed openly without requiring employees to bring them up through the informal organization. This should be done even when managers don't agree with the solutions being proposed, thereby demonstrating their openness to ideas and their personal integrity.

Managers who are willing to give employees' ideas a try even when they disagree are respected as democratic, visionary, and trustworthy by the employees they supervise. This openness builds trust and support for those managers within the informal organization of the group. It makes practical experience the decisive factor rather than emotional speculation, and employees take increasing responsibility for company outcomes as a result. Although managers are ultimately responsible for the solutions they select to address problems, they should be prepared to go along with solutions they feel are not optimal as long as no serious harm to the organization or its members is likely to result. By implementing employees' ideas whenever possible on an experimental basis, they build the trust necessary to request that employees conditionally accept unpopular managerial directives.

Discussion of the process for implementation of an idea or plan must of necessity focus on what will actually be done, who will do it, and when—in other words, the action steps. When employees participate in the development and revision of action steps, they fully own the outcome of their effort. Contention and resentment are eliminated by having employees report on their progress as they implement the action steps for which they are responsible. After assessing their progress, the manager and the workgroup may revise the action steps, add to them, or refine them. As the workgroup's visions are realized, everyone can take pride in his or her contribution to the success of the group.

Employees should be helped to understand that action steps are preliminary suggestions for how to proceed to make the visions for the company reality. If employees feel that they will be bound to complete a certain step without having an opportunity to make adjustments in it, they may withhold their support.

This resistance is a common reaction to their fear that they have agreed to a measure that is not in their best interest. Ongoing participation in the development of action steps required for the realization of both company and employees' objectives insures full cooperation and maximum coordination. Both management and the informal employee organization can openly acknowledge that when new ground is broken, everyone is learning at the same time. The improvement of implementation plans through revisions is an expected part of every strategy used to optimize the collective effort of the work environment.

Active employee participation in the implementation and monitoring of change fosters ownership, teamwork, trust, and self-respect. In short, continuous communication between employees and management regarding the goals and visions of the informal organization generates and maintains support within the informal organization while employees become effective problem solvers.

> **Managers can maintain continuous communication and maximize coordination and communication in the workplace by doing the following:**
> 1. **Review visions.**
> 2. **Encourage action.**
> 3. **Maintain communication.**

1) Review Visions

Communicating with employees is what managers routinely do on an ongoing basis. However, what is being suggested here is a very special form of communication. Most routine managerial communication deals with implementing the directives of management. While this affects individual employees, it does little to manage the informal organization of employees as a separate entity. Employees have a special interest in the issues they identify during a listening activity. They have a vested interest in the goals and visions they develop and a desire to make the changes necessary and do the work required to make their visions reality. Typical managerial communications do not capitalize on the energy these factors generate.

No additional meetings are necessary to empower managers who have completed the processes discussed previously. They simply need to take a moment in regular meetings to review employee visions, request volunteers to take the suggested action steps, congratulate employees who report success, and ask for assistance in revising visions that cannot be realized. After reviewing the outline of employee visions, the manager only needs to request volunteers to pursue some of the action steps. Employees may choose which visions to address. Of course, visions that are easier to address are often selected first, and this provides early successes for the group.

Employees volunteering to work on action steps may suggest additional steps and modifications to existing steps as the need arises. They are requested to pursue the required actions with the assistance of their manager and report their progress at the next regular meeting. This provides managers with an opportunity to work directly with their employees on projects that are personally important to them. If no one volunteers to work on a vision and undertake the identified action steps, the vision will simply remain a vision. It happens occasionally that no volunteers come forward to take the steps necessary to bring a vision into reality. Morale will be unaffected in these situations because the group is simply deciding not to pursue what it previously thought to be important.

2) Encourage Action

As employees volunteer to pursue the action steps they have identified, they will find themselves working with other employees and possibly other executives within the company. Employees gain important information and insights from doing the research and legwork required to implement action steps. In most situations, they need managerial approval prior to making any changes they identify as necessary to achieve their visions. When approval can be given, management is viewed as supportive. When it cannot and the reasons are explained, employees learn more about how the company's interests are intimately related to their own. Managers can provide assistance, encouragement, and recognition for members of the group who accept responsibility for working toward improvement. When employees request direction and advice, managers should assist them without taking ownership of the process or outcomes. Managers are merely acting as resources and advisors in these situations and should assist the members of the group only when asked and in the ways suggested.

It is important to acknowledge that the group's visions, and the work they do toward fulfilling them, are important to the company because they reinforce employee ownership of processes and outcomes. Allowing employees to drive progress on action steps invites them to apply their special knowledge and creativity to mutual problems. It should be clear that the realization of employees' visions is a company priority that will be pursued to the greatest extent possible under the particular situation in which the company finds itself.

3) Maintain Communication

Once a manager has led employees through processing their concerns, it is necessary to maintain the mutually supportive relationship that results. This is done by maintaining continuous communication regarding employee visions and progress. Keeping channels of communication open helps preserve the support of the informal organization. As employees discuss the implementation and modification of their visions with management, they are processing their emotional reactions to the workplace in a constructive way. They are meeting their needs for status, recognition, and purpose at the same time. Managers who take the time to maintain communication regarding employee visions forge lasting and supportive relationships with those they supervise.

Managers should celebrate with employees every time action steps are successfully taken. Each action step brings an employee vision closer to reality within the company. The realization of these visions is tantamount to creating an ideal workplace in their eyes. The hope and thrill generated by making progress on such projects releases employees to be creative and to care about other company objectives. After all, if the company doesn't succeed, there will be no workplace to improve. Managers should recognize the work done and congratulate the members of the team who have successfully taken a step toward improving the workplace. Managerial recognition reinforces the status of supportive employees and provides opportunities for others to be acknowledged as well. Working on behalf of others is a cause that transcends merely working for wages because it meets higher-order needs.

To the extent possible, it is advantageous to encourage employees to pursue the more easily attained visions first to provide frequent and early successes. Each success builds confidence and loyalty to the company. Success also encourages others to risk accepting responsibility for working on behalf of their peers. Success breeds success. Potentially, problems could arise when the group's goals cannot be met because they require unavailable resources in terms of time, money, or material, or are based on unrealistic expectations. When employees desire to use inefficient methods to revise long-standing company policies or strategic plans, there is no reason for alarm. These situations are relatively easily addressed by management regardless. When there is disagreement concerning what should be done, a pilot program or experiment can be conducted to address points of disagreement over method. This will ensure that disagreements are settled by the law of the situation rather than by authority, power, compulsion, or compromise.

When issues, goals, visions, and action steps are developed by the employees, a strong sense of ownership is inculcated from the outset. Employees and management jointly have the challenge and responsibility for identifying solutions to problems arising within the company. The work to make visions reality brings employees into intimate and personal contact with the rationale of managerial activity. When problems arise, it is not management's role to solve them. Managers cannot abandon the mission or engage in irresponsible conduct simply because employees desire it. They can, however, attempt pilot programs and experiment with employee ideas to determine empirically whether ideas and suggestions are practical. When they are not, employees do not blame managers and managers do not blame employees. On the contrary, managers and employees alike are validated and feel respected as contributing members of an organization that is more important than any one of them individually.

4) The Historical Foundation of Continuous Communication

In the early 1900s, Frederick Winslow Taylor noted that his then revolutionary concept of scientific management was not based on any unprecedented ideas, nor on any new invention or startling discovery. Instead, it amounted to a new combination of basic elements of management. Taylor simply collected information, analyzed it, and combined it into what he called scientific laws and rules that were made effective by changes in attitude on the part of workers and management.

He conceived of the success of scientific management as hinging on changes in attitude that affected relationships and interactions in the workplace.[142] The attitudes of workers and managers ultimately affect their approach to one another, their duties, and their responsibilities. Although many of those who attempted to implement scientific management neglected it,

---

142   Taylor, The Principles of Scientific Management, 122.

Taylor always stressed the indispensability of continuous communication between management and employees.[143] He cited good communication as the single most important factor in reducing friction between managers and employees. Frequent and personal contact between a manager and his or her employees sets the stage for close, sustained cooperation. Continuous communication prevents discontent from building up behind the scenes and spreading among employees. It is difficult for people to maintain a quarrel when they share the same interests, work together day after day, and engage in authentic discussion of the real issues facing them.

In the 1920s, Mary Parker Follett underscored some of the reasons continuous communication is required for ongoing success. It's reasonable to question why it is necessary for managers to maintain communication with employees regarding their visions and progress in taking action once the development process has been completed. The answer lies in the ever-changing character of the work environment. Follett noted that employees' interactions with one another stimulate continuous change in the companies for which they work. There are three levels of change:

(a) The workplace impacts and changes the employees.
(b) The employees impact and change the workplace.
(c) The employees impact and change themselves.

Each of these factors affects the others and is affected by the others in turn, thus creating a very complex environment.[144]

This constant state of change and response to change affects employees' desires, concerns, goals, visions, and actions. Continuous communication improves the reaction of employees

---

143 Ibid., 125.
144 Follett, "Relating: The Circular Response," *Mary Parker Follett Prophet of Management*, 50-51.

to change by reducing stress and providing opportunities to integrate their interests with those of the company. In fact, open and efficient communication processes make it possible for the objectives of informal employee organizations to be integrated with those of the company. In the absence of such processes, cooperation is nearly always impaired and communication patterns and styles actually become more dysfunctional.

The workplace is not static. New personnel, processes, customers, deadlines, techniques, informal social structures, and any number of factors are constantly modifying it. Employees react to these changes both consciously and unconsciously and trigger additional changes in their environment and their own behavior. When a supervisor asks an employee to undertake a new task, he may respond in a variety of ways. Whether he is happy about the assignment or annoyed, he responds to the change brought on by his supervisor's request. If he expresses annoyance, the supervisor may react in such a way that his interactions with other employees could be affected.

Not only that, but the supervisor may hesitate to give the employee other assignments based on his reaction to the first request. Even the simplest interactions produce changes that ripple through the social structure of the informal organization. If even a fraction of these interactions are powerful enough to actually modify the desires of the workgroup as a whole, its visions will require at least some type of addition or revision. These adjustments are necessary to maintain the support of the informal organization. Continuous communication regarding matters of special importance to employees is necessary to maintain their support. It is useful to remember that any issue of importance to the informal organization must be of importance to the company of which it is a part if there is to be an ongoing integration of interests and objectives.

Follett always conceived of coordination within companies as a necessarily continuous process of communication.[145] Managers

---

145   Follett, "The Process of Control," *Mary Parker Follett Prophet of Management*, 221.

shouldn't wait until a crisis happens to begin discussing workplace issues. Instead, the coordination of management and the informal organization should be an ongoing activity. Although it takes very little time to confer with employees when things are running smoothly, the benefits are substantial in terms of employee perceptions of management. Open communication allows employees to air their concerns, which greatly attenuates the power of the employee "rumor mill." When employees feel certain that their managers will listen to their questions and concerns, they will approach their managers directly rather than rely on inaccurate and inflammatory gossip.

Managers who are on friendly terms with their employees and who frequently touch base simply to learn how things are going are perceived as personable and accessible. When difficulties arise, discussions will be necessary of course, but employees will not feel that the only time managers want to speak with them is when something is wrong. Managers come to be viewed as members of the team and allies in the joint effort to create a better future for everyone. Power struggles between managers and employees cease because everyone shares the same interests.

A significant advantage of continuous communication is that the planning and evaluation required for coordinated effort is continuous as well.[146] Activities cease to be considered in isolation. The work itself becomes the reference for evaluating the functioning of the department or company. Both management and employees are working to improve the ongoing activity of their organization rather than merely surviving serial crises. This broader perspective eliminates unreasonable demands and encourages moderate approaches to disagreements.

Employees deal with change better in work environments characterized by open and continuous communication. In the absence of this, changes are much more disruptive and require much more time for employees to adjust. Adjustment periods are often

---

146   Ibid., 222.

characterized by conflict and dramatic decreases in efficiency. When employees are free to discuss their reactions to changes and the issues they raise, the work of the organization continues with minimal lost time and opportunity. Employees acquire a broader perspective of the company and the role they play when communication is continuous. They tend to view changes in the workplace as less disruptive and threatening.

As situations change, everyone must work together to keep pace with those changes. Employees affect the direction of changing situations depending on how they view them. When they view change positively as a professional challenge, they find their work interesting and rewarding. Problems become opportunities to meet their needs to be creative. However, changes viewed as threatening encourage employees to become defensive; when that happens, they communicate less and show greater resistance to management directive. Continuous communication is necessary to maintain employee support because change is an ongoing process. Consider, for example, the adjustments required of employees when new technology is introduced by management. The new technology is introduced to solve problems; however, once it is introduced, the situation is changed for the employees involved and fresh problems emerge. New problems require additional communication to prevent employees from taking their insecurities underground where they can fester unchecked.

People working together pass from situation to situation seamlessly. Continuous communication helps dispel the dysfunctional misconception of problems as being discrete events. A given problem cannot be considered in isolation without inviting the belief that solving the problem will be the end of the employees' difficulties. Problems occur continuously. Communicating with employees regularly fosters the sense that problems are normal and will always occur. They are a natural outcome of sustained, coordinated effort. Rather than solving individual problems once and for all, employees and managers come to realize that they are managing a stream of problems to maintain the efficiency of their company.

Managing the stream of problems successfully is necessary to the success of every company. Workgroups that maintain continuous communication develop the ability to respond to the problems that inevitably arise quickly, calmly, and efficiently. Employees acquire a sense of confidence and satisfaction in being members of workgroups that function as successful teams that can maintain their efficiency in the face of challenging circumstances. Everyone values being an important part of a winning team. Effective communication allows employees to maintain efficiency in the face of adverse circumstances that quite possibly would disrupt other companies.

In the 1930s, Elton Mayo made a number of discoveries through his research at the Hawthorne Plant of the Western Electric Company.[147] He found that the output of the workers in the test room continued to increase over a period of three years before leveling out at a record high. Amazingly, the gains in productivity were independent of experimental changes arbitrarily introduced during the research period. Employee productivity and morale did not decrease when negative events were introduced as part of the research study. Employee efficiency was unaffected by events that had a detrimental effect on other employees.

The researchers at Hawthorne were puzzled by the sustainability of the improvements in the test room and attributed it to a lasting change in attitude on the part of the employees. The employees themselves reported that they felt free of conditions that interfered with the work of other departments, but they were unable to specify the cause of their positive attitudes toward the company and their work. Mayo noted that they showed greater resistance to adverse circumstances than other workers. For example, when experimental conditions returned to what they had formerly been within the department, there was no significant

---

147   Mayo, *The Human Problems of an Industrial Civilization*, 170-171.

decrease in output or morale. In other words, the attitude of the employees was quite stable and supported the continuation of higher productivity in the face of the adverse conditions they introduced in the workplace.

One experiment involved giving employees in the test room and those in another department a special privilege. After productivity had stabilized, the plan was to withdraw it with the expectation that productivity would return to previous levels once the incentive was removed. As predicted, the morale and productivity declined immediately with the withdrawal of the privilege in the department serving as an experimental control. But to the amazement of researchers, morale and productivity remained unchanged in the test room.

To discover the differences between the test room and the other departments within the plant, Mayo's researchers interviewed twenty thousand persons over a two-and-one-half-year period. If the differences could be discovered, a dramatic increase in productivity and morale could be sustained despite future situational changes that employees might perceive as negative. At first, the interviews were aimed at investigating differences in supervisory practices applied in the test room and those utilized in the remainder of the plant. Researchers pursuing this found that employee statements about supervisors were not sufficiently reliable to justify any sort of changes in managerial policy within the plant. If the researchers were to find differences in managerial practice, they would have to find another way to obtain useful data rather than interviewing the employees themselves.

Finally, researchers in the Hawthorne plant identified the differences between employees in the test room and those in other departments had to do with their attitudes. Employees outside the test room were plagued by a sense of futility and loss of freedom while employees in the test room reported a sense of hope and personal freedom. Mayo concluded that the stability of employee morale and performance in the test room could not be explained in terms of factory organization and executive policy alone. Sources of resistance to adverse events within departments would need to be attributed to social disorganization and a sense that employees were unimportant and somehow irrelevant within the context of the company.

The only documented difference between the test room and other departments was the presence of ongoing communication between managers and employees. In the test room, communication was continuous and employees felt important and connected to the company. The researchers asked the employees how they felt about a variety of aspects of their work environment, and they listened attentively to their responses. The communication conducted continuously in connection with Mayo's research was itself determined to have significantly altered employee attitudes and increased their toleration for adversity in the workplace. This effect, known to this day as the Hawthorne Effect, is so powerful that it continues to be indispensible to the study of research design. Continuous communication is the key to managing the informal organization and maintaining supportive employee attitudes.

In the 1940s, Chester Barnard emphasized the key role executives play in the communication process. Managers maintain operations within their companies by maintaining formal communication.[148] Since operations are continuous, it follows that the best communication processes are continuous as well. However, managers tend to focus on the formal communications of management while neglecting communication with the employees they supervise. Informal communication processes dramatically affect the level of support of informal organizations of employees. When communication is safe, open, and continuous, managers find themselves supported by their employees. When the channels are damaged, employees will not identify with the mission of the company.

In the 1950s, Norman Maier urged managers to work harder to understand employees' views rather than to try to convince

---

148   Barnard, *The Functions of the Executive*, 215.

them to agree with management. To do this, he advocated creating a climate conducive to discussions regarding employees' feelings about the issues that concern them. Managers should prime employees for these discussions by raising issues that they know are of concern to the group.

For example, if a manager is aware that employees are angry about a new company policy, the manager should bring this up and list it along with any other issues of which she is aware. After the manager starts the list, the employees can be asked for help in completing it. The focus becomes the creation of a comprehensive list of issues facing the employees and the company in an atmosphere of openness. Once a number of painful issues have been raised and the manager has shown that she is not defensive, employees will be more willing to share their views freely. In the absence of this opportunity, they will be sharing their views on the policy among themselves in the manager's absence. Underground discussions create rumors and damage morale through misinformation. As hostilities increase, even normal communications between the employees and the manager will grow increasingly dysfunctional. Giving employees a chance to vent without repercussions strengthens the working relationship between the manager and the participants. Getting all of the negative feelings out on the table prevents them from festering behind the scenes and interfering with the work of the department or company.

After the list is complete, the manager should ask employees if the policy has merit. Although the employees may feel that a policy does a very poor job of addressing an issue, they may acknowledge at least a few good points if they feel they have been heard. If any favorable points are mentioned, the manager should note them as well. If not, she should acknowledge that the employees have raised serious issues and let it go at that. She should not try to convince employees of the value of the policy by defensively recounting what management views as its merits. Once employee concerns have been heard, the problems raised by the policy can be addressed by management and employees working together. The issue is no longer whether management has the power and legitimacy to impose the new policy, but how the problems that policy was designed to address can best be solved.

Maier called this the two-column method.[149] He believed that providing an employee with the opportunity to express two sides of an issue was indispensible to problem solving in the workplace. Free discussion allows employees to explore the facts behind their disagreements with management and allows management to address problems in fluid situations where the actual problems are difficult to define. Continuous communication with employees is necessary because employee attitudes play an important role in the way they select and organize facts. In other words, employee attitudes actually determine the meaning of facts and events. This means that management's view of the facts can be expected to have little impact on employee opinions. Direct attempts to bring employees' views in line with those of management are not successful because there is disagreement over the relative importance of considerations as well as the facts themselves.

When managers allow employees to discuss the issues they find important without defensively and dogmatically referencing the facts, they allow employees to define disputes for themselves and critically examine the significance they have given to them. This is not possible in mutually defensive discussions in which managers present their facts and employees respond by presenting their own.

Inviting employees to discuss troublesome issues after priming them brings the emotional issues of the informal organization into the open. Asking them if they are aware of any positive aspects of situations following a complete listing of their concerns invites them to consider the matter more globally without defensiveness. Even if they refuse to offer any positive statements, the

---

149   Maier, Solem, and Maier, *Supervisory & Executive Development*, 80-81.

reevaluation process has begun for them. This is one of the great strengths of Maier's two-column method.

After managers have listened, problem solving can begin by having employees determine certain goals and define them with visions. Employees will understand the complexity of their problems better when they develop action steps to make their visions reality. This process manages attitudes, not by controlling or manipulating them, but by providing employees with an opportunity to engage in cooperative problem solving with management not otherwise possible.

Employees are not able to cooperate with management in the absence of the support of their informal organization. Negative attitudes cannot be directly examined or challenged by management. They can only be managed through processes that demonstrate that management understands and respects the feelings behind employee responses to their working environment. Employees are free to examine and change their attitudes only when the needs to defend and protect them have been removed by continuous, meaningful communication with management.

Communication processes change as the relationship between the informal employee organization and management improves and matures. After the channels of communication have been opened, regular meetings with employees become less tense and formal. Comments regarding negative conditions may be made without any intent that they be addressed. In some situations, employees merely want to be recognized for the sacrifices they are making and their contribution to the welfare of the group. When issues are raised, the employees discussing them will informally work together to find solutions. As this becomes more frequent, the manager's role moves more and more toward that of advisor and facilitator and away from that of an authoritarian overseer. When negative situations result from managerial directives and changing conditions, employees will band together to make the department successful. Flawed strategic plans become interesting challenges that employees make workable despite the problems involved.

Essentially, each of the processes of listening to identify issues, to set goals, to develop visions, and to identify action steps will become more informal and less time consuming as the informal employee organization views its objectives as consistent with those of the company. The continuous communication that results provides a full range of opportunities for employees to meet their self-actualizing needs as they pursue company objectives. The efficiency realized through employee creativity and self-motivation can be astounding.

Managers who have achieved continuous communication enjoy working with their employees rather than being in conflict with them. They creatively engage their employees in the work of the company. Virtually all issues arising in the workplace are addressed through communication that includes the manager and his or her employees. Employee suggestions are taken seriously, and they are implemented in a spirit of experimentation to find the best way for both management and employees to address the ongoing challenges of the modern workplace. Informal employee organizations participate in the successes and failures of the company and become something of a social unit that meets the higher-order needs of employees through the support of the company. Employees acquire a sense of working for a greater cause, and the good of the group takes on increased importance.

10.

MANAGING INFORMAL ORGANIZATIONS

Most people spend nearly one-third of their lives between the ages of twenty and sixty working to earn a living. Those who have fulfilling jobs are happier and enjoy more productive lives than those who are unhappy with their jobs. People who suffer in the workplace carry the residual effects of their misery to nearly every other aspect of their lives. Improvements in the quality of the workplace are not only desirable from an ethical point of view but also from a business perspective. The effective management of informal employee organizations will increase the efficiency, productivity, and profitability of any business. Supportive employees can reduce the cost of goods sold, improve product quality, and minimize repair and replacement costs.[150]

It is often a concern of management that allowing employees to set their own goals to deal with their own issues can raise expectations for control of the processes and planning that are typically within the purview of management. Mangers fear that the employees may raise demands that management cannot realistically meet, with the result being loss of control and even lower employee morale. This is not the case. The concerns of informal employee organizations center on meeting the higher-order needs of their members such as the need to perform important work and attain status among their peers. Employees pursue and will continue to pursue the satisfaction of their needs regardless of any interven-

---

150   Michael G. Aamodt, *Applied Industrial/Organizational Psychology*, 3rd ed. (Belmont: Wadsworth Publishing Company, 1999), 2.

tions management may attempt. Managers may only choose to facilitate the integration of employee objectives with those of the company, or they may tolerate the lack of cooperation and soldiering that plague companies in which informal organizations of employees are ignored.

When employees develop their own goals and visions through the communication processes discussed herein, they become more effective in their work because they own those goals. When employees pursue their own visions, they meet their higher-order needs in the context of pursuing the mission of the company. Managers are not responsible for pursuing the visions employee develop. Their task is simply to facilitate employee efforts to improve their workplace by providing guidance and support. If management were to actually take on the responsibility of pursuing the goals identified by employees, the process would fail. Employee participation in problem solving is an indispensible ingredient of effective management. Employees must be led to articulate their problems, define them, brainstorm solutions, and pursue effective solutions.

The communication processes described in this book provide opportunities for management to formally acknowledge that employees have issues, and then to provide them with avenues to pursue solutions that are consistent with the objectives of the company. This allows managers to be viewed as facilitators who care about employees and who do whatever they can to improve the workplace. In most instances, employee visions can be realized. When employee goals cannot be met, employees realize that the specific circumstances of the company are to blame rather than an uncaring manager.

These processes also provide a means to address the everyday conflicts that inevitably arise when groups of people need to work together and cooperate. When employees object to the directives of management, managers can respond by listening and acknowledging employees' perspectives. When employees are led to develop goals and visions, they can work toward realizing the changes they desire by pursing the action steps they develop. This almost always involves research on the part of employees to discover the facts and the true rationale behind the offending directives. Research conducted by employees has great credibility within the employee ranks. Once the exigencies of the situation that generate unacceptable directives are known, employees are empowered to creatively explore alternative approaches to addressing the objectives of the directives. This frees management to amend the directives as both employees and managers share the objectives of the offending directives.

In the rare instances when their attempts to deal with an issue fail, employees are not frustrated and do not blame management. Dealing with issues in the workplace is viewed as a joint venture—a kind of team sport, so to speak. Achievement-oriented managers sometimes misunderstand that the higher-order needs of employees are met during the problem-solving process itself even if the specific problem being addressed is not solved. When the informal organization is managed effectively, employees view managers as allies.

In the early 1900s, Frederick Winslow Taylor cited worker productivity as the single most important factor in the prosperity of nations. At that time, average workers in developed nations were five or six times more productive than those in undeveloped nations were. Despite this, Taylor felt that even in developed nations, the greatest cause of unemployment was employees deliberately restricting output. He attributed this to the widespread belief held by workers that it was not in their interest to work as hard as they could.[151] This belief developed within the informal employee organizations and proved to be very resistant to management's attempts to refute it. In the absence of a process capable of influencing the attitudes of employees positively, the opposition of the informal organization to management's quest for increased efficiency is the rule rather than the exception.

---

151   Taylor, *The Principles of Scientific Management*, 124.

The need to consider the informal organization in the execution of plans developed by management does not lead to any significant loss of control. Mary Parker Follett defined control as power exercised by managers to achieve specific ends.[152] Managers acquire their power only nominally from the authority that the formal organization gives them. Power and authority are not the same. It is through recognizing that managers need the goodwill of the informal organizations within their departments and plants that the opportunity to develop real power emerges. By acknowledging the weakness of management and developing employee support through improved communication processes, managers can increase their power to deal with the situations that confront them.

Follett advocated reliance on the law of the situation rather than authority to legitimize managerial directives. When both employees and managers are governed by the shared commitment to deal with the situation rather than to exert power over one another, great things happen.[153] The relationship between employees and management is revolutionized. A team is born. In the absence of this, employees and managers are in a sort of competition to gain power. Much energy is wasted as each side attempts to increase its power through manipulation, diplomacy, collective sabotage, and even violence. The competition itself takes its toll on morale on both sides and leaves a damaged, inefficient communication process in its wake.

The result is quite different when management helps employees discover the law of the situation. When this is done, there is no need for either group to garner power over the other to pursue company objectives. The situation itself dictates what needs to be done, and the members of both groups cheerfully meet the challenges that emerge. Follett advocated abandoning the race to acquire power in favor of developing power that can be exercised

---

152   Mary Parker Follett, "Power," *Mary Parker Follett Prophet of Management,* ed. Pauline Graham (Washington D.C.: Beard Books, 2003), 101.
153   Follett, "Constructive Conflict," *Mary Parker Follett Prophet of Management,* 107.

jointly. Rather than management's attempting to acquire power over the informal organization or vice versa, both groups understand that they exert power *with* each other in addressing the situations that confront them as they pursue the mission of the company.

To develop power *with* employees, managers need to abandon their quest for attaining power *over* them. This can be done by integrating the interests of both the informal organization and management and by agreeing that both groups should submit to the law of the situation.[154] When this is done, employees can be given a certain amount of authority over their contribution to the combined endeavor of the company. Simply abdicating the responsibility of management by giving all authority for decision making to employees is not what is being advocated here. Authority should never be delegated prior to developing methods for employees to take responsibility for the authority they are given.[155] Before giving employees authority over any portion of the decision-making process, managers must engage them in pursuing company objectives, and their interests must be integrated with those of management.

The integration of interests ensures that employees will be guided by the law of the situation rather than by narrow, selfish considerations. In the absence of this integration achieved through skillful communication, the power of the informal organization is divorced from the mission of the company and will be exercised unconsciously. When employees have an emotional stake in the success of their company, they can be expected to make high quality decisions that promote their own interests and those of the company at the same time. If management requests a sacrifice from employees, anger and hostility will naturally follow because the employees will view such a request as an attempt by managers to exercise power over them. The law of the situation depersonalizes such adverse occurrences. When both managers

---

154   Ibid., 108-109.
155   Ibid., 112.

and employees study the situation to see what it demands, sacrifices are volunteered rather than demanded. There is a world of difference.

When the situation demands a sacrifice, the issue of commanding and obeying does not arise. There is no one to blame. The situation just *is*. Managers and employees become concerned with identifying the best way to deal with an impersonal situation to further their mutual interests. Orders are viewed as coming from the situation rather than management. Both groups accept the situation at face value. The problem shifts from the question of whether management has the authority to issue an order to what the best order should be.[156] Employees realize that they can issue directives to managers just as managers can issue directives to them.

This happens easily and naturally in companies with active, supportive informal organizations and when employees are consulted for suggestions regarding how to accomplish a novel task or implement a troublesome directive. Suggestions by employees are implemented if they address the situation better than management's directives are able to do. If orders are depersonalized by reference to the law of the situation, most complaints from employees regarding dictatorial bosses will cease.[157] Managers should not be afraid to exercise their authority in appropriate circumstances, but by allowing their authority to come from the situation, they can improve their relationships with their employees.

Changing the emphasis to gaining control of situations rather than of the people involved profoundly alters the dynamics of the workplace. Managerial directives are no longer viewed by employees as arbitrary commands. Employees connect with one another and with management in new ways as they respond to changing situations as a team. Issuing commands without allowing employees to become full partners in a situation through appropriate commu-

---

156 Mary Parker Follett, "The Giving of Orders," *Mary Parker Follett Prophet of Management*, ed. Pauline Graham (Washington D.C.: Beard Books, 2003), 128.
157 Ibid., 129.

nication does a great deal of harm.[158] Discussion allows employees to discover the law of the situation and fully support the organizational response to it. The communication processes that engage the informal organization define not only employee attitudes but, to some extent, the meaning of the situations themselves.

Consider for example the handling of mistakes. If managers consider mistakes to be the products of laziness and negligence, censure and blame are often the result. Finding those responsible for the error and imposing punishments or reprimands may seem appropriate as a form of corrective action, but censure damages relationships. Not only is the relationship between the manager and the employee damaged, but the relationship with the entire informal organization is bruised when the employee talks about the experience with coworkers in the absence of the manager.

If the mistake rather than the employee is considered the problem, the situation becomes the controlling factor and different responses become appropriate. The question of how best to deal with the error becomes everyone's focus. Managers and employees will band together to deal with a problem rather than a person. How to correct errors and prevent them from recurring becomes the focus.

Orders should be depersonalized through communication processes in which managers and employees discover the law of the situation together. Employees can be educated regarding the techniques of their jobs to reduce the number of directives management feels compelled to issue. Finally, reasons can be provided when directives are given, and alternative approaches to dealing with situations can be considered.[159] This encourages the informal organization and management to attack challenging circumstances as a team. In the absence of an engaged informal organization, attempts to educate employees will be viewed merely as management's exercising its authority over employees. In com-

---

158. Ibid., 130.
159   Follett, "The Giving of Orders," *Mary Parker Follett Prophet of Management*, 131.

panies with supportive informal organizations, the education provided by management is viewed as recognition of the indispensible role played by employees in the success of the company.

This is not to say that directives should be discussed every time they are given.[160] On the contrary, directives are often issued to save time. There is no need to provide reasons when managers can reasonably assume that employees are already aware of the situation and therefore they agree with the directives. However, reasons are very helpful when new or unusual directives are issued. The advantage of this over the expectation of blind obedience is that managers are able to discover and deal with any resentment before it can interfere with the work of the organization. Hostility that goes underground increases in intensity and damages the relationship between management and the informal organization. Employee resentment increases in situations where their perceptions cannot be processed.

Consider for example a situation in which a manager is directed to award a modest bonus to the most productive employee in the department. The alleged purpose of the bonus is to reward the most productive employee and inspire less productive employees to increase their efficiency. Immediately, the manager has a problem. No matter which employee receives the bonus, the others in the department will be angry with the manager for not recognizing their worth. Rumors will spread regarding how and why the particular employee was selected. What can be done if the manager is not in a position to challenge this inept attempt to increase production?

The answer lies in telling the truth and discussing the situation openly with all of the employees involved. This depersonalizes the directive and shares the responsibility for the outcome of the situation with the workgroup. Allowing employees to express their resentments and other feelings regarding the directive will strengthen the relationship between the manager and the employees. When the manager follows the suggestions offered

---

160   Ibid., 132.

by the employees in awarding the bonus, he will not be driving the resentments underground or devaluing any of the employees in his department. He will be viewed as simply doing his job. The employees who shared in the decision regarding who should receive the bonus will feel valued. The discussion process has successfully focused the attention of the group on the situation rather than the fairness of the manager's decision, and the informal organization remains supportive of the manager.

When managers involve employees in situations, they are not perceived as imposing their will when decisions are made and actions are taken.[161] They meet their employees' needs for being respected for the contributions they make within the company. Even though the roles of the manager and the employees differ, employees feel that they and the manager play different but complementary roles in the same endeavor. Situations that otherwise could have been divisive become occasions for mutual support and actually strengthen supportive attitudes within the informal organization.

The best leaders show employees what must be done and train them to think for themselves.[162] They foster leadership among the employees who work for them. Without giving up their power, they energize the people who work for them and enable them to help the organization progress to new levels of efficiency and productivity. Great managers define employees' responsibilities through continuous communication and provide them with the training and equipment necessary to meet their responsibilities. Rather than persuade them to blindly follow managerial directives, they lead rather than drive them in the common pursuit of company objectives. By integrating employee interests with those of the company through the communication process and by assisting employees in making their visions reality, managers can teach employees to think for themselves rather than to expect manage-

---

161   Ibid., 134.
162   Mary Parker Follett, "The Essentials of Leadership," *Mary Parker Follett Prophet of Management,* ed. Pauline Graham (Washington D.C.: Beard Books, 2003), 173.

ment to do their thinking for them. As employees pursue their visions along with the company objectives to which they relate, they become leaders themselves.

Workgroups benefit from diversity.[163] Understanding the communication processes that align employee interests with those of the company frees managers to be more tolerant of diversity within their departments. No longer are managers faced with the need to ignore differences with a view to minimizing friction within their departments. With confidence in their ability to use disagreements to increase efficiency within their workgroups, managers are in a position to take advantage of diverse viewpoints and cultural backgrounds.

Unfortunately, the problem of maintaining wholehearted collaboration between the informal organization and management has persisted despite advancements in management theory and practices.[164] Management traditionally defines problems in economic terms, such as identifying low productivity and attempting to increase it by offering economic incentives or imposing economic sanctions. This approach disregards the human factors that actually underlie underperformance.

Managers need to become effective listeners who can react appropriately to whatever they hear in dealing with company problems.[165] In the absence of training, most managers are unable to relate to employee concerns involving non-economic issues. Unfortunately, emotional and status issues profoundly affect the performance of most employees. The ability to use effective communication processes allows managers to access the creativity and goodwill of employees. When managers know how to listen, they can lead employees in formulating appropriate responses to their concerns that will enhance their contributions to the company.

In the absence of communication processes capable of integrating employee objectives with those of the company, much

---

163   Ibid., 179.
164   Mayo, *The Human Problems of an Industrial Civilization*, 179.
165   Ibid., 183.

employee potential remains untapped because employees do not share a common purpose with their companies.[166] Although most managers believe their employees should share a common purpose with management, this is almost never the case. Individual motivations are internal to each employee and carry an emotional load, while company purposes are viewed as external and lacking significant emotional meaning. However, an exception to this occurs when company purposes become sources of personal satisfaction for the employees. When this occurs, individual motivations to further their own interests provide the impetus for employees to pursue company objectives. Although rare, this phenomenon can sometimes be observed in connection with work for family, patriotic, and religious organizations.

The reason for this lies in the primary purpose of companies engaged in business for a profit. In such companies, the practice is to make up any insufficiency with respect to non-material inducements for employees with material inducements, such as bonuses and commissions.[167] However, substituting material for non-material satisfactions is effective only for a limited time and to a limited extent. Monetary rewards are inadequate to induce cooperative behavior in the long term. For companies pursuing purely economic objectives, non-economic inducements are important to the continued efficiency of operations. Employees must be able to satisfy their higher-order needs while pursuing company objectives for any durable and efficient cooperation between management and employees to be established.

Unfortunately, providing non-economic incentives such as prestige and respect is not an easy task for management. Establishing conditions that encourage individual pride can be inconsistent with encouraging the cooperation necessary to a team effort. Maintaining the delicate balance between the individual and the group so that higher-order needs can be met in the workplace requires

---

166   Barnard, *The Functions of the Executive*, 88-89.
167   Ibid., 93-94.

management of the informal employee organizations that have evolved there. Informal organizations exercise increasing influence as companies grow. The larger a company is the more impersonal its systems for coordinating human effort become. The motivators on which they rely are based on an economic logic not shared by most employees. The larger a company becomes, the more managers tend to rely on official communications consisting primarily of directives delivered to employees impersonally. Employees are influenced by their emotional reaction to the workplace at least as much if not more than the expectations of management.

In business organizations especially, the focus on making profits naturally leads to attempts to make up for the lack of non-material incentives by substituting material incentives. While this may be successful to a limited extent for short periods, the idea that material incentives by themselves can maintain the cooperation necessary for high efficiency goes against human nature. Non-economic inducements are vital to establishing and maintaining productive efficiency.[168] These inducements can be provided only through effectively managing the informal organization through communication processes capable of allowing employees to address their concerns in the context of company objectives. Effective communication coupled with the legitimization of employee interests in non-material, non-economic elements of the workplace integrates their objectives with those of the company. A fully engaged informal organization can meet the higher-order needs of employees and promote cooperation at the same time, thus allowing employees and management to share common purposes.

Managing the informal organization does not involve management giving up its responsibility for directing the operations of the company. Effective management does not mean that employees will always be satisfied. Having employees make all of the decisions will not increase efficiency, and higher levels of employee satis-

---

168   Ibid., 94-95.

faction will not, by themselves, necessarily increase productivity.[169] What is necessary is that the informal organization be permitted to pursue its objectives at the same time employees pursue company objectives. For example, if employees desire longer breaks or cleaner lunchrooms, or more input into decisions regarding the assignment of personnel to certain tasks, they should be allowed to explore the economic, physical, and legal reasons for maintaining the status quo.

Suggestions regarding how to make their visions of the ideal workplace reality should be taken seriously and implemented whenever possible. Increases in employee efficiency may make longer breaks possible while reducing company costs at the same time. Employee assistance in maintaining a cleaner lunchroom may increase morale and reduce cleaning costs at the same time. Considering employees' desires regarding their assignments may increase morale and motivation at the same time. The integration of objectives requires that the interests of both the company and the employees are considered legitimate.[170] This means working together to make the company successful for the benefit of all—employees, managers, shareholders, and customers.

Managers make decisions based on assumptions they have regarding their employees.[171] They acquire these assumptions from their experiences in the workplace. Not only do these assumptions color the approach managers take in dealing with their employees, but they also influence employee-manager relations. Negative assumptions produce employee behavior that confirms them, while positive assumptions result in employee behaviors that justify trust and make full cooperation possible. Much of the literature available to managers today is based on assumptions consistent with Douglas McGregor's Theory X and can be summarized as follows:

---

169   McGregor, *The Human Side of Enterprise*, 64.
170   Ibid., 71-73.
171   Ibid., 45-47.

1. Most employees dislike work and will avoid it if they can.
2. Because of this, managers must coerce, control, and direct them to secure the cooperation necessary to successfully pursue company objectives.
3. Most employees prefer to be directed because they dislike responsibility, have little ambition, and value security above most other considerations.

These assumptions have predominated within management due to their emphasis in the literature. Managers accepting them have experiences with employees that reinforce their negative view of human nature. When employees respond to management practices based on these assumptions, they withhold full cooperation and have little investment in company objectives. To improve efficiency and profitability, managers should base their practices on the assumptions McGregor called Theory Y:

1. Working is as natural to people as play or rest. Most employees do not inherently dislike work. In companies in which the informal organization is properly managed, work can become a source of satisfaction for employees that voluntarily contribute their best effort.
2. External rewards and punishment are not the only means for securing employee cooperation. Employees will pursue objectives to which they are committed without external controls.
3. The commitment of employees can be secured by making the appropriate rewards available in the

workplace. The satisfaction of egoistic and self-actualizing needs is the most powerful motivator for inducing employees to pursue organizational objectives.

4. Most employees will not only accept responsibility but will seek it.

5. Appropriately motivated employees have a high capacity to use imagination, ingenuity, and creativity in solving organizational problems.

6. Most companies are only partially utilizing the intellectual, creative, and productive potential of their employees.[172]

Modern employees are primarily motivated by self-actualizing needs. Management cannot provide self-respect, status among peers, or feelings of self-fulfillment for employees. It can, however, create conditions within the informal organization that encourage and enable employees to fulfill these needs as they contribute to the missions of the company. These conditions are created through communication processes that are designed to allow the informal employee organization to align its interests with those of the company. Managing the informal organization is not the same thing as controlling it. On the contrary, the communication processes described merely free employees to support their companies. If managers are not genuinely concerned with their employees' welfare, some of their employees will simply leave the company rather than cope with this on a regular basis.

McGregor's Theory X, management by direction and control, falls short in motivating employees because it is based on satisfy-

---

172   McGregor, *The Human Side of Enterprise*, 65-66.

ing basic human needs.[173] Incentives of this sort are of relatively little value in motivating people whose important needs are social and egoistic. Depriving employees of opportunities to satisfy these needs at work results in exactly what might be expected. Frustrated employees often seem lazy, disinterested, hostile, and combative. It is natural for them to resist change and leadership imposed by a manager who is not only unaware of what is important to his or her employees, but who presides over the communication processes that actually prevent this information from coming to the surface.

Opening the channels of communication sufficiently to allow the informal organization to integrate its objectives with those of management requires an involved process—at least initially. Once those channels have been opened, a change in orientation will take place within both the employee and management ranks, which will allow issues to be handled much more informally. Managers who take the time to improve communication will be rewarded with increased efficiency and lower stress. The processes capable of improving communication and managing informal employee organizations are summarized as follows:

The Processes in a Nutshell

(Chapter 5) Managers can facilitate the identification of issues by listening to their employees. This is accomplished with the following steps:
1. Meet with the employees.
2. Prime the group and ask for help.
3. List the issues.
4. Set a time to address the issues identified.

---

173   Ibid., 54-55.

(Chapter 6) Managers can facilitate employee goal setting in the following way:
1. Review the issues.
2. Categorize concerns.
3. Develop goals.

(Chapter 7) Managers can facilitate the development of positive visions of the company within their employees by doing the following:
1. Review the goals.
2. Envision the ideal.
3. Share the vision.

(Chapter 8) Managers can facilitate the development of action steps by employees by doing the following:
4. Revisit employee issues.
5. Identify action steps.
6. Integrate the vision.

(Chapter 9) Managers can maintain continuous communication important to managing the informal organization by doing the following:
7. Review employee visions.
8. Encourage action.
9. Celebrate successes and facilitate revisions.

What is being advocated here is a change from standard management practices that typically ignore the informal organization altogether. Rather than attempting to identify powerful employee motivators based on the latest conceptual framework, simply create an atmosphere open to communication and ask the employees themselves. This will eliminate much time, misunderstanding, and stress on the part of the employees and management. Rather than attempting to control employees and drive them toward company objectives, enlist employees in pursuing joint objectives through open communication. Employees will communicate among themselves regarding every action taken by management. Managers can only choose to ignore or participate in that conversation.

In companies that have opened the channels of communication, debates over who is responsible for doing the work or responsible for failures are replaced by managers and employees working together to find the best way to deal with the situations that confront them. Managers are free to help employees creatively contribute to the team effort in ways that satisfy their self-actualizing needs while they are pursuing company objectives. Employee creativity and dedication are resources that every organization can harness with appropriate attention to the management of the informal organizations that inevitably exist within the formal structures created by management.

BIBLIOGRAPHY

Aamodt, Michael G. *Applied Industrial/Organizational Psychology*. 3rd ed. Belmont: Wadsworth Publishing Company, 1999.

Barnard, Chester. *The Functions of the Executive*. 13th Anniversary ed. Cambridge: Harvard University Press, 1968.

Bass, B. M. "Does the Transactional-Transformational Leadership Paradigm Transcend Organizational and National Boundaries?" *American Psychologist,* 52(2), 1997, 130-139.

Bishop, J. W., & Scott, K. D." How Commitment Affects Team Performance." *HR Magazine,* 42(2), 1997, 107-111.

Crosby, Philip B. *Quality without Tears: The Art of Hassle-Free Management*. New York: McGraw-Hill, 1984.

Feigenbaum, Armand. *Total Quality Control*. New York: McGraw-Hill, Inc., 1991.

Garske, G. G. "The Relationship of Self-esteem to Levels of Job Satisfaction of Vocational Rehabilitation Professionals." *Journal of Applied Rehabilitation Counseling,* 27(2), 1990, 19-22.

Graham, Pauline, ed. *Mary Parker Follett Prophet of Management*. Washington D.C.: Beard Books, 2003.

Howell, J. M., & Avolio, B. J. "Transformational Leadership, Transactional Leadership, Locus of Control, and Support of Innovation: Key Predictors of Consolidated-Business-Unit Performance." *Journal of Applied Psychology*. 78(6), 1993, 891-902.

Hunt, J. W., & Laing, B. "Leadership: The Role of the Exemplar." *Business Strategy Review,* 8(1), 1997, 31-42.

Judge, T. A. "Does Affective Disposition Moderate the Relationship between Job Satisfaction and Voluntary Turnover?" *Journal of Applied Psychology,* 78(3), 1993, 395-401.

Judge, T. A., & Watanabe, S. "Individual Differences in the Nature of the Relationship between Job and Life Satisfaction." *Journal of Occupational and Organizational Psychology*, 67, 1994, 101-107.

Judge, T. A., Locke, E. A., Durham, C. C., & Kluger, A. N. "Dispositional Effects on Job and Life Satisfaction: The Role of Core Evaluations." *Journal of Applied Psychology*, 83(1), 1998, 17-34.

Juran, J. M. *Managerial Breakthrough.* revised ed. New York: McGraw-Hill, 1995.

Maier, N.R.F., Allen R. Solem, Ayesha A. Maier. *Supervisory & Executive Development.* New York: John Wiley & Sons, 1957.

Mayo, Elton. *The Human Problems of an Industrial Civilization.* 2nd ed. Cambridge: Division of Research, Graduate School of Business Administration, Harvard University, 1946.

McGregor, Douglas. *The Human Side of Enterprise.* annotated ed. Joel Cutcher-Gershenfeld. New York: McGraw-Hill, 2006.

Mullen, B., & Copper, C. "The Relation between Group Cohesiveness and Performance: An Integration." *Psychological Bulletin*, 115(2), 1994, 210-227.

Newsome, M., & Pillari, V. "Job Satisfaction and the Worker-Supervisor, Relationship." *The Clinical Supervisor*, 9(2), 1992, 119-129.

Podsakoff, P. M., MacKenzie, S. B., & Ahearne, M. "Moderating Effects of Goal Acceptance on the Relationship between Group Cohesiveness and Productivity." *Journal of Applied Psychology*, 82(6), 1997, 974-983.

Repetti, R. L., Cosmas, K. A. "The Quality of the Social Environment at Work and Job Satisfaction." *Journal of Applied Social Psychology*, 21(10), 1991, 840-854.

Taylor, Frederick Winslow. *The Principles of Scientific Management.* New York: Harper & Row, 1911.

Yuki, G. A. *Leadership in Organizations.* 3rd ed. Englewood Cliffs, NJ: Prentice Hall, 1994.

Made in the USA
Charleston, SC
03 October 2013